Para
mis queridos amigos
Sylvia y Joe Baltrona,
love

Antonio Castillo de la Gala
February 29, 2020

HAPPINESS

is a

FUNNY BUSINESS

A practical guide to help you achieve a sense of happiness,

well-being, and harmony in your life.

Plus, some fun stories of my life.

Antonio Castillo de la Gala

Printed in the United States of America

First Printing, 2019

Print ISBN: 978-1-54399-650-0

eBook ISBN: 978-1-54399-651-7

TABLE OF CONTENTS

Foreword   1

PROLOGUE: Why I Wrote This Book   3

CHAPTER I - Does Everybody Want to Be Happy?   7

CHAPTER II - Gratitude   14

CHAPTER III - Love and Family   24

CHAPTER IV - Inconveniences   27

CHAPTER V - Perspective   33

CHAPTER VI - Cell Phones   41

CHAPTER VII - "Here Comes Santa Claus"   46

CHAPTER VIII - Don't Rain on My Parade   50

CHAPTER IX - Calisthenics for Your Mind   52

CHAPTER X - Not Tonight, Dear...   56

CHAPTER XI - Have You Ever Sung a Song on a Public Bus?   60

CHAPTER XII - Race: Check the Appropriate Box   67

CHAPTER XIII - "Play It Again, Sam"   70

CHAPTER XIV - Christmastime...and Other Times Too   73

CHAPTER XV - Caressing   77

CHAPTER XVI - Time Flies When You're Having Fun or Time's Fun
When You're Having Flies   79

CHAPTER XVII - Tennis, Chess, and Old Age   82

CHAPTER XVIII - "Where there is music, there can be no evil." — Cervantes, Don Quixote   90

CHAPTER XIX - T.G.I.F.? More Like T.G.I.T.   94

CHAPTER XX - The Genie in the Bottle (*Carpe Diem!*)   101

CHAPTER XXI - No Mexicans on TV!   107

CHAPTER XXII - A Beggar with a Stick   111

CHAPTER XXIII - Les Misérables   115

CHAPTER XXIV - *Peccatum Minuta*   118

CHAPTER XXV - From Veracruz to the Beverly Hills Hotel   121

CHAPTER XXVI - Motivation and the Next Mountain   128

CHAPTER XXVII - "How Do I Get to Hollywood?"   132

CHAPTER XXVIII - Giving Is Happiness: A Christmas Story and Other Tales of Kindness   135

CHAPTER XXIX - To Date or Not to Date…   141

CHAPTER XXX - Silence Is Golden   149

CHAPTER XXXI - Happy Holidays and All That Jazz   152

EPILOGUE: Some Closing Thoughts on This Business of Happiness   155

Endorsements   165

This book is dedicated to my family, friends, acquaintances and the thousands of persons who listened and still listen to my talks about happiness.

A very special dedication to my Grandmother Elena Porragas de Rodriguez de la Gala, my Grandfather Francisco Rodriguez de la Gala Guerrero, my Mother Maria Elena Rodriguez de la Gala de Castillo, my Father Antonio Castillo Azueta, my Brother Francisco Castillo de la Gala and my Brother Jorge Castillo de la Gala. They are all gone from this world and I miss them very much but they truly live in my heart. Thank God, my Brother Javier Castillo de la Gala is still with us. All of them helped me, at different times, to become the man that I am today.

Last, but not least, my son, Antonio Castillo, III, which is my pride and joy. My latest source of incredible happiness are my two grandchildren, Antonio Castillo, IV and his brother Alexander Castillo.

Foreword

Dear Antonio,

I love your book! Not only is it full of fun, engaging stories about your amazing life journey...it's also full of wisdom.

Your chapter on Gratitude is my favorite. (You might recall that Gratitude is the first of the "magical words" in my book *The Wisdom of Merlin.*)

Well done, my friend. You have come a very long way from that little fellow called "Chopincito"! And you've earned every bit of your great success. Now you are passing on to others your ideas about how to find happiness — which makes this book both enjoyable and important.

All best wishes,

T.A. Barron

Author of The Merlin Saga,
an international best-selling series

Nothing is impossible to a willing heart.

John Heywood

Why I Wrote This Book

After spending so many years giving advice and sharing my ideas about happiness with relatives, friends, acquaintances, strangers, and almost anyone who would start a conversation with me, I felt it might be fun and worthwhile to put my perspective in writing. That way, my ideas could be more widely accessible to a greater diversity of individuals. In other words, I thought that maybe a book could allow me to reach even more people and help them find happiness. Also, this book is a testament to my philosophical thoughts.

Some time ago, friends began to tell me things like: "You know, Antonio, I find it hard to believe that you are consistently in such a good mood — you're always so cheerful and you express a nonstop positive attitude." Some began to wonder whether I was "full of it," or perhaps even more surprisingly, whether I might be for real.

You see, more than 30 years ago I made a life-transforming decision: I chose to embrace and build my now-well-known positive attitude. From that important moment forward, I have noticed many remarkable benefits. As a pianist who always values the next gig, I've been able to honor all the performance engagements I've been given the opportunity to fulfill throughout my five-decade career (knock on wood). And beyond my annual physical exam to reconfirm my good health, I have had little need to see a doctor in my many years (knock on wood again — harder!). Each day that I am given to live and breathe on this earth seems like a precious present to me. I am filled daily with a sense of joy and bewilderment and I appreciate the wonders of everyday life from the moment I wake up each morning to the moment I close my eyes to drift off to sleep at night.

To achieve this state of mind, spirit, and body that my family (with one exception) and friends have come to admire, I needed to make some changes in the way I looked at my life. I was not born seeing life through rose-colored glasses; I made a conscious decision, just as life offers each one of us choices every day. I realized that each day can either be a struggle just to get through or a joy to experience. I can't tell you how thankful I am that I chose the latter.

By following just a few disciplined daily principles and practices, you too can discover the capacity to truly transform your life. I know this to be true, because it happened within me, and others have noticed the positive difference. And I have proven (through my "scientific experiment" of one) that the joy of living is sustainable...even after more than 30 years.

The principles and practices I follow on a daily basis work, and they are quite easy to implement. Ultimately, a content and joyful state of being, simply requires the *discipline and commitment to be happy*. Believe it or not, the inner transformation begins right then and there, just by repeating to yourself the simple phrase "I want to be happy" — and meaning it.

Antonio Who?

I was born in Veracruz, Mexico, to a beautiful family, including my mother, father, grandmother, grandfather, and my three brothers, Francisco, (RIP) Javier, and Jorge (RIP). We were not well-off by American standards — we had no television at home and only occasionally did we have access to a telephone. Our prized possession was a half-broken "*ortofonico*," an archaic-sounding word that my grandmother coined to reference our very old record player, which had a charming crank at its side and on which my grandfather would play both classical and opera recordings from his now-collectible records...well, I'm sure they *would* be collector's items if my brothers and I had not come up with the brilliant idea to use them for target practice with our BB guns and slingers!

I can now see, with the benefit of hindsight, that it was precisely our lack of TVs, phones, and certainly Internet access that led my brothers and I to become so much closer to our parents and to each other than if we had had such distracting, though world-expanding, resources. I believe that our bond with one another was far stronger than many children today enjoy with their parents and siblings, judging from my limited observations. To this day, I treasure the fact that we built a community and everlasting connection to one another through our shared passion for music, books, conversation, and, above all, family.

When I think of my childhood home, my very first memory is of the baby grand piano that graced our living room. It was a beautiful black Knabe that had brought music into my family's hearts since my grandmother was a child. I think that piano had been in our family since the late 1800's! My lifelong passion for the music which, in my view, the piano alone can uniquely evoke, began at the young age of three. In fact, I gave my first performance in kindergarten, or the *Jardin de niños* #1. Amazingly, I still can remember what I played for my audience of five-year-old peers, their parents and our teachers. It was an old Mexican song, "*El Gavilán Pollero*" ("The Chicken-Hunting Hawk").

My grandmother, Elena Porragas de Rodriguez de la Gala, who was my first piano teacher and an endless source of musical inspiration, had a spirited sense of humor, which I am blessed to have "inherited" from her. It was through her joking around with everyone, that we understood ourselves to be truly loved for exactly who we were, and it was through her love, that we sought early on to become our best selves in the process of growing up. In her honor, I have tried to infuse my music with a light-hearted sense of joy, balanced by the profound impact that sublime melodies and arrangements can inspire in sensitive souls. So, I suppose the seeds of my happy approach to life were first sown by my grandmother, who had a great influence over me.

After completing high school in Veracruz, I moved to Mexico City to study at the National Conservatory of Music, where I graduated as a concert pianist with the highest degree they conferred — the equivalent of a Ph.D. in the United States.

I guess there are moments in each of our lives when we have to actively decide to try to advance and grow. For me, this was one such moment. I felt that I was not growing as an artist and that my career was going nowhere in Mexico. After pursuing a career as a concert pianist for several years as well as performing in a band I had formed along with my brothers, I made one of the most momentous decisions of my life, I decided to move to the United States of America.

America has provided me with so many unbelievable opportunities and blessings that it would be impossible to name them all. We truly live in the land of opportunity. Believe me when I tell you it is not a mere coincidence that this land is the birthplace of my philosophy of happiness and my disciplined attempt to make every day genuinely count.

CHAPTER I

Does Everybody Want to Be Happy?

Happiness, n. An agreeable sensation arising from contemplating the misery of another.

— *Ambrose Bierce*

A couple of times, people have asked me "What is happiness to you?" I understand that most people probably don't need to define that feeling, as they likely feel either happy or unhappy. I always tell them, that happiness, in a nutshell, is the feeling of being satisfied, full of positive emotions, having joy in my heart and peace in my soul, and of being fully aware that I have never intentionally harmed another person in my life. I have an almost complete absence of negative thoughts and emotions and very little stress. As a matter of fact, a few years ago, I took a stress test along with a lot of people working at a hotel where I was performing. I did it just for the fun of it. The person conducting the evaluation told me that he had never seen such a low score in the stress results. I wasn't surprised. I am filled with calm and the never-ending belief that everything is going to be OK.

The first time I read the Ambrose Bierce quote above, I thought, "What a curmudgeon." But sometimes I wonder if Mr. Bierce had a point. Let me tell you about Mr. and Mrs. Curmudgeon.

For 11 years, I played the piano five days a week from 11:00 a.m. to 2:00 p.m. at Macy's Plaza in downtown Los Angeles. Playing there for all those years, as well as in many concert halls, hotels, restaurants, shows and private homes, and talking to probably thousands of people around my piano, has been, and remains, a great joy. My experiences have given me an exceptional understanding of human nature by observing the varying philosophical approaches to life of countless people from so many different backgrounds. Say what you will about Los Angeles, but it is certainly filled with interesting people!

In my opinion, Los Angeles is a city that has one of the best climates in the world. Only every so often, a little — and very welcome — rain falls here, clearing the air and making everything smell fresh again. I mention this because it caused me to notice something, that I thought was strange. Sometimes on those rainy days, people would walk up to my piano and, before even saying hello, begin saying how much they hated the rain, and how depressing it was for them.

For a while, I tried to explain to those people that in a place like Los Angeles, where it doesn't happen very often, rain provides welcome relief and a refreshing change of atmosphere. But there was simply no reaching most of them. Some people will hate the rain even if it is as sporadic as it is in L.A. Remarkably, I noticed similar behavior during the nearly perennial sunny days. There was always someone in the crowd who would say something like, "I always hate these sunny days; why can't we have some rain?" Actually, for all I know, some of those people could have been the very same complainers I mentioned before!

You get the point. To some people, the glass will always be half empty. To me, it's always half full. For instance, I think that the sound of rain falling outside can make playing Chopin even more poetic. The rain makes my mood more nostalgic and it provides a lovely background to the music.

If it is sunny, the weather is perfect for a game of tennis. If it's cold, somehow my mind goes to my favorite time of the year, Christmas. It's all about perspective.

Speaking of Christmas, every year, as soon as the malls put up the decorations, I hear more curmudgeons. They say things like "I don't like this time of year" and "Can you play something other than those silly songs?" I have heard these complaints every year at my piano, even though I only play Christmas music from the day after Thanksgiving until Christmas day. Well, to be honest, I play Christmas carols until January 7th. In Mexico, as in many countries all over the world, January 6th is the day when children get their Christmas presents. In Egypt, Georgia, Russia, Serbia and the Ukraine, the children get their presents on January 7th. I still remember how exciting was for my brothers and me the evening of January 5th; we could hardly go to sleep, the sense of anticipation very hard to describe. A great majority of people would smile at the sounds of the first Christmas carol they heard, and I could feel the warmth of their greetings. But there were always a few complainers.

The same can be said about the decorations in the mall. Most people would smile at the first sign of them, saying, "I can't believe it is that time of year again!" or "I'd better start my shopping." Again, there were also the complainers ("I don't like the decorations this year!") and, of course, the "everything in the past was better" crowd.

You probably know who I'm talking about. We all know someone like that. They're the eternal complainers. The ones who, when talking about a film, will say something like, "In my day, movies were better." Such contempt is not limited to cinema. Perhaps you are also familiar with these gems: "In my day, children behaved better," and "In my day, music was better." And so on.

I always tried and tried to please these people, and I would point out the pleasure in enjoying the present. I love that word in the English language: the present. It is indeed a "present" to all of us. It is a lovely gift. I don't waste my time or energy in comparing the present with the past or obsessing over what the future may bring.

When I tell complainers that in "their day" a lot of children died very young because of a lack of advanced medicine, they quiet down. I also love to play music for these eternal complainers that was written in recently. Knowing they enjoyed it, I then reveal the truth to them about the song's age. They usually dismiss it by saying, "Well, I am sure that was an exception."

Try it my way. When I see the decorations in the mall, instead of complaining about how much nicer they may have been in the past, I appreciate the fact that we have them at all. Instead of complaining about how movies aren't as good as they used to be, I try to find the enjoyable new ones, and believe me, there are plenty of them around. The same goes for music and anything else. It's a simple choice: You can either waste your life lamenting and making people around you feel miserable, or you can be grateful for the fact that you are alive and can enjoy things that are only a dream in many parts of the world.

A few years ago, I would frequently visit a friend of mine who owned a Mexican restaurant in Westwood, which is a nice neighborhood in Los Angeles. Many nights, after I finished playing the piano at the Beverly Hills Hotel, I would go to his place, where he, a couple of other friends, and I would play dominoes or poker for a few dollars. We enjoyed great conversation in the grand old tradition of Mexican men getting together, with roughly 70% of the talk focused on politics and philosophy and 30% on women.

Sometimes, I would go to see this friend of mine during the day while he was getting ready to open for business. Typically, I would walk in and say, "Good morning!" to which he would retort, to my amusement, "There's nothing good about this morning!" He was in a grouchy mood most of the time.

We're still friends today, and when we talk about those days, we get a kick out of it, especially because I tell him, "You know, every time that I left your restaurant, I was happier and felt better than when I walked in."

It's funny, I think. Maybe in a subtly sadistic way, we sometimes feel better about our lives once we hear of somebody else's misery. By the way, my friend doesn't own that restaurant anymore. He is a successful attorney. Talk about misery!

So, can this be? Can people really garner happiness from other people's misfortunes? If so, why? And here's a question that's even more interesting: Does everyone *want* to be happy?

One day, I was discussing the idea of happiness with people who were gathered around my piano. I said to them, "Everybody wants to be happy, right?" To my surprise, one person in the group answered, "No; I don't want to be happy." He continued to explain how he believed that feeling blue made him more aware of being alive. I couldn't understand such a feeling. I asked him what kind of music he liked, and he uttered, "I only enjoy listening to the blues." What a coincidence.

That reminds me of another story from a few years ago. I was playing at the world-famous Hotel Bel-Air in Los Angeles, at a time when they still permitted smoking in the bar (They banned it in 1999, thank God). I went up to the bar to refill my glass with water (I drink water the whole night while I play piano). While I was waiting for the bartender, I saw a lady looking at me with a cigarette dangling from the side of her mouth. Her head was sort of bobbling up and down. It reminded me of the little toy dogs in the back of cars that you can see moving their heads up and down, up and down. She was staring at me and I had the feeling that she wanted to say something to me. Finally, I looked right at her. Then she asked me, in a raspy, throaty kind of voice, "Do you play the blues?" Before I had a chance to answer, Steve, the bartender, told her, "No, he can't; he's an optimist."

I am not going to imply that everybody who listens to the blues is a pessimist, but I found it kind of funny that the man from the previous story loved the "blues." And that lady who started a conversation with me later said, "Sometimes I just kind of like to hurt, to feel sad, to feel pain. Don't you?" I told her the truth, "No, I don't like to hurt; I don't enjoy pain and I love being happy." She gave me a look that I read as saying "Get out of here," so I happily went back to the piano.

I've talked to probably thousands and thousands of people around my piano while playing at hotels, restaurants, concerts, recitals, shows, and malls (more about that later), and similar topics usually come up with the people that approach me. Many people comment on how I really seem to love my work. That usually sparks an animated conversation concerning one of my favorite subjects: career goals and happiness. While I believe that the great majority of people whom I have encountered in my life would love to find happiness, I have come to accept the fact that a few of them don't find the concept of happiness very appealing.

Somebody told me long ago that the idea of being happy was boring to him. He mentioned something about how the state of being happy was not "a fertile ground for creativity." I am paraphrasing here, but that was the gist of what he said. Another lady that I met a few years ago told me, "Happiness is like a fairy tale because it's never true."

I am sure that their idea of happiness was shaped by their personal experiences or perceptions of life, just like my own. I guess some people are just wired differently.

The notorious curmudgeon Aldous Huxley wrote, "I can sympathize with people's pains, but not with their pleasure. There is something curiously boring about somebody else's happiness." That quote reminds me of a particular acquaintance of mine who told me a few years ago, "I can't stand Mozart's music; it's too happy!"

Sometimes when I interact with these types of people, my happiness tends to throw them off. One lady I went on a few dates with, tried to explain to me that I wasn't really happy, that I was only deceiving myself. Another lady I went out with a couple of times told me over the phone, "I can't go out with you anymore. I don't believe in happiness and to see you acting happy all the time makes me believe that it's all a mask, not for real; therefore, I don't think that you are for real." She hung up on me and I never heard from her again.

Oh well. I guess we have to accept that the concept of happiness means different things to different people, and that it's just not 100% accepted by or even appealing to everybody's way of thinking. But reconciling our own experiences with others is a constant theme in life.

For instance, I used to foolishly think that everybody loved classical music, but of course throughout the years I have met individuals who really don't enjoy it. That doesn't mean that I think something is wrong with them or that I can't relate to them at all; it's just that different people have different tastes formed by their wonderfully different experiences. Personally, I do not enjoy rap "music" (an oxymoron, in my humble opinion) or the blues, and I don't think there's anything wrong with me either.

If you are the kind of person who enjoys feeling sad, hurting, listening to the "Why did you leave me" or the "I am going to die without you" kind of music, this may not be the right book for you. On the other hand, you might be pleasantly surprised and find something useful for you, something that you might relate to.

So, if you're one of the unlucky few who do not believe in happiness, please keep reading anyway. You might be happily surprised (sorry about that —couldn't resist).

CHAPTER II

Gratitude

*Gratitude is the most important part
of keeping a positive attitude and
understanding the business of happiness.*

This chapter will focus on what I call "walking around being grateful." Over the years, this humble piece of advice has triggered the most responses from people. Some have told me that it has given them a different way of looking at life and has helped them travel the road towards happiness. Let's take it from the beginning.

One morning, many years ago, I woke up feeling that things were not working out very well in my life. While taking my usual long shower, I was feeling sad about how my career was going nowhere, with no sign of progress at all. I was also feeling sad thinking about my ideals and my wish to make a difference in my life, with which I was making apparently little progress. My dreams of becoming a concert pianist and touring around the world were not materializing, and my music composition seemed to have hit a dead end. To make matters worse, I didn't have a love life to speak of.

The desire to have a full and complete life kept coming back to me. I knew that to make myself feel better, I would need to be a positive influence in other people's lives, whether it was with my music or some other idea.

Then one day I said to myself, "Stop it! You have no right to complain or feel sorry for yourself." It was time for change, so I started taking a personal inventory of my life up to that moment. Pretty soon, the mental balance was tilting more and more towards the positive, productive, and happy side of the scale, to the point where I started to feel more energetic, optimistic, happy, and *grateful*.

From that moment on, I started to develop a kind of system or methodology that I enacted in my daily life. My first baby step was simple. Each morning when I woke up, I would say out loud to myself, "I am happy that I woke up today."

Pretty simple, huh? My thinking was that by waking up, the odds of reading my name in the obituary section of the paper would be considerably low. As silly as it may sound to you, that simple thought — my gratitude for being alive — gave me exactly what I needed to start the morning in a positive direction.

After a while, I went from being grateful to be alive, to being happy to see another day, to sleep with a roof over my head and to be able to breathe on my own.

Once it started to flow, my gratitude could not be stopped. I started feeling grateful while I was taking my hot showers, appreciating how really nice it is to be able to take a long hot shower whenever I would like to. Such a simple pleasure wasn't always available to me. I remember how, while growing up in Veracruz, Mexico, my mother would have to prepare the hot water, and how even then we would have only a few minutes before the water would start to get cold. With such a method of showering, daydreaming was not a good idea. If I got lost in my thoughts about music, life, goals, or any of the countless thoughts that can pop into one's head, I would find myself running out of hot water very soon and hurrying to rinse before the water was too cold to handle. Now, while taking my long, hot showers here in the United States, I think back to my childhood days and realize how lucky I am now to not have to worry about being shocked by cold water. Such a simple thing, right? But wonderful, nonetheless.

The element of gratitude, which I think too many people never even give a second thought, helped rejuvenate my enthusiasm each day and let me start each morning on a happy note. From then on, practicing gratitude became a daily mental routine that I still do to this day, even as I'm writing this book. Once I started feeling grateful, I began to recognize more and more things to be grateful for. Sometimes the littlest things can be simply wonderful.

For example, I started to feel grateful about having a nice bowl of cereal with a cold glass of milk every morning. My favorite way to have my cereal is to mix two kinds — one "healthy" kind and another with more flavor and crunchiness — in a bowl of milk. I put the bowl of cereals and milk in the freezer before jumping (actually, I don't jump, just walk) in the shower. That way, when I'm ready to have my breakfast, the top of the milk in the bowl is frozen and I have to break it with my spoon. Then I pour some honey, sprinkle some nuts, add a little banana or blueberries or strawberries, and I'm in cereal heaven. I read many years ago that athletes in the early Olympic Games would drink honey to boost their body's resistance and endurance. I don't know if it's true, but from that day on, I've always poured honey on my cereal.

After all these years, the only change in my daily morning routine is that now, instead of regular milk, I use almond milk. I guess it is healthier and in Los Angeles, where I live, everybody is a health guru. A lot of people walk around with bottles of water under their arms. I guess some of that rubbed off on me. But the cereal is as far as I will go with the almond milk. By the way, I always think that it's very funny that it's called almond "milk", I know that the definition of milk is a fluid that is produced by the mammary glands of mammals. For a good old-fashioned milk shake, nothing beats regular milk. Actually, I always order malt, chocolate malt. OK, I'm getting pretty hungry here! Ah, the little things. After a few years of milk and honey in my cereal, I now have freshly squeezed orange, tangerine or grapefruit juice, directly from the trees in my yard, along with a nice yogurt. A few times a week I have a good shake of almond "milk" with fresh strawberries, blueberries, protein powder and ice. Delicious.

I'm sure you can imagine how this continued to develop, how my gratitude spread and spread without end. I started feeling grateful that I had a car. Actually, that thought still makes me feel happy. I remember very well how, as a child, I would look out the window to the street and watch the cars go by. I remember thinking how very, very difficult it would be to ever save enough money to be able to buy one. Many years later, when I moved to Mexico City to study at the National Conservatory of Music, I would look at the parking lot of the school and think about how grateful the students who owned cars must have felt. Usually, from the different places that I lived all over Mexico City, it would take me three different buses to make it to the Conservatory. That would mean getting up a heck of a lot earlier every day, not to mention being caught out in the rain or cold. And let me tell you, it rains a lot in Mexico City, and in the winter, the cold cuts through your sweater like a knife.

In all honesty, I don't remember ever being upset that I spent most of my years at the Conservatory without the luxury of an automobile, as my father used to call it. I remember many nights, after all of the lights had been turned off one by one (I was usually the last student to leave school), the night janitor, Don Alberto, a very sweet and decent man, would come to my cubicle, where he would find me practicing night in and night out. He would say the same words to me every evening: "Antonio, I have to close the school, time to go home." I would then walk out with him to the main gate of the Conservatory and then we would say good night.

From there, I would walk to the nearest bus stop, which was a few blocks away from the school. In wintertime, or on rainy nights, it wasn't what you would call a fun walk. But as silly or unbelievable as it may sound to you, I don't remember complaining ever to anybody, including myself and God, about the fact that I didn't have a car. I guess I was too busy feeling very grateful about having the opportunity to play my piano. In those days at the Conservatory, I didn't have a piano at home, so practicing at the school was essential to keeping my fingers in shape and my dreams alive.

When I finally got my own car, of course I was grateful, but it didn't stop there. I continued to notice the little things as well as the big things, like having a daily meal, and a mind able to understand music, and an unlikely good memory for music (everything else is not that easy for me to remember). I was grateful for having a job, and enormously grateful for being blessed with a healthy child. You get the picture. One morning I decided that I would count the situations that made me feel grateful throughout the day. By the time the afternoon came around, I had counted 57!

So now I guess I don't even have to consciously remember to be grateful. It's now like a habit of mine that I won't ever break. For me, walking around being grateful is as natural as breathing, thinking, eating, and sleeping. I never seem to stop being asked the same questions: "Antonio, how come you are always happy?" and "You always seem so happy — how do you do it?"

Friends, family, and acquaintances have told me for years that I am the happiest person they know. I have also heard on more than one occasion, "You're always so happy it makes me sick," and "You're full of it — nobody is that happy!"

In an e-mail I received a few years after we had broken up, an ex-girl-friend of mine wrote, "Sometimes I wanted to hit you in the head, because I just couldn't imagine how in the world you could be happy all the time." Lucky for me, she never did hit me in the head. Today, she is still my friend, and I even played at her wedding in 2004.

But I do see her point. It's not that sadness hasn't been a part of my life. I have had plenty of sadness and suffered both emotional and physical pain on many occasions. Who hasn't? I am a human being. I have had my share of tribulations, pains, heartbreaks, and disappointments in my personal life and in my career. I just do my best to shake it off and focus on the good things.

Gratitude has played a big role in how I can work through the unpleasant parts of life and remember all the reasons I have to be happy. It doesn't matter how small the reason is: a meal, a snack, a drink. Sometimes I'm grateful to get a small break from work, when I can read and escape my obligations (playing the piano, writing, composing, or just taking care of business) for an hour. I am *always* very grateful for that moment. And then, when I am working, well, I'm grateful then too because it has always been my dream to play the piano for people. I can't imagine not being grateful because all I have to do is think back to the days when such simple pleasures were luxuries.

Growing up in Veracruz, Mexico, we didn't have a lot of what you might consider material riches. There were no TV sets or stereos in our house, and using a telephone and riding in a car were only occasional treats. However, we did have plenty of food, companionship, books and great conversations. We had a roof over our heads, and we had good schools and plenty of love and attention from our parents and, while they were alive, our grandparents.

When I moved to Mexico City and entered the National Conservatory of Music to pursue my goal of becoming a concert pianist, I founded myself with some big problems ahead of me. To begin with, my parents did not have a lot of money to send to me, so, at first, I stayed with a family who were friends of my parents. The problem was solved, for a short time, but then I still needed to buy books and pay for my transportation to school.

Many days I woke up knowing that I didn't have enough money for breakfast. On those days, I wouldn't eat until lunchtime at the Conservatory, and only then because I had a punch card that I had won in a piano competition which allowed me to have one lunch every day, five days a week. The incentive to try to win that small competition, which I did, year after year, also fueled my energy and desire to practice harder. Without that meal card, I have no idea what I would have done for food.

Looking back on those days, I feel that they made me a much stronger person. I don't remember ever complaining to my parents or to God. Every time my parents wrote to ask me if everything was OK, I always replied yes, that everything was fine and great. I figured that there was no need to worry my mother any more than she already did. She was always worried sick about my three brothers and me.

When I think back about those days at the Conservatory, or about the rainy days in Mexico City, or about running as fast as I could to catch the next bus, or about those cold winter days with my flimsy, old sweaters, believe me, I am reminded of countless reasons to be grateful every single day. Things used to be different, and it's very easy for me to remind myself of all the blessings that I have in my life now. Being grateful is now a way of life for me, and gratitude itself is something I have long considered to be a major factor in the happiness equation.

I'd like to ask you to try a little exercise. It's simple and it can be done any time you have a free moment, like before you go to bed, or before you continue on to the next chapter in this book. Think of as many little details in your life from the past 24 hours, or even from the past week, and try to identify the situations that you think warrant being grateful for. Try to count them all.

I have a pretty good idea of what might be going through your mind. Don't you see how long the list could be? It would be very, very hard not to come up with reasons to be grateful, whether it is the fact that you ate today, or that you have shelter, or that you have people who love you, or even that you have the capacity to read this book.

Perhaps tonight, right when you are ready to go to sleep, you can try this little experiment again, but more thoroughly. Go through your whole day and be grateful for every little thing that's right and good, right down to the smallest, most seemingly trivial details. Going back over your day, from the moment that you opened your eyes in the morning to the moment that you lay down to go to sleep, you are going to be amazed and surprised at the list's length. You'll probably find so many things the number of reasons you have to be grateful will be overwhelming. Such a realization is an important step on the road to true happiness. You'll start to see that when there are so many good things around you, how could you not be happy?

Try this exercise again a second day. And a third. And so on. Soon, you'll be well on your way to changing your whole attitude about life. You can do it your way, but I find it most rewarding to begin with the moment I first open my eyes. Say to yourself, "I am happy to be alive and to have the opportunity to experience another day and to try to do something positive with my life." It might give you that extra buzz that I hear coffee gives to some people in the mornings (I'm not a coffee drinker myself).

After a few days or weeks of doing that small exercise, take the next step and add something else to your daily routine. When you take your morning shower, which I am assuming you do, be aware of the hot water running down your body. Be conscious of how nice it feels. As I told you before, I take pretty long showers in the mornings. I love the feeling of the hot water on my body, but I also like having the relaxing opportunity to say out loud everything that I feel grateful for so far in the day. For me, it is the time to daydream and think about goals and music and remind myself of all the good things in life.

By the way, these little exercises can even be accomplished while you do your daily errands. With practice, these positive thoughts will become part of your daily routine, but only if you have the commitment to do it every single day. Personally, I cannot recall a day when I don't stop to recognize situations that make me feel grateful.

I'm sure that you get the idea. I think you will be amazed at how much you can be grateful for when you just take the time to consider it. Pretty soon, you will look at life and the world around you with different eyes. Eventually, your friends and family will start taking notice of these changes. I have heard countless times, from people who come up to my piano while I am playing, or from friends getting in touch by telephone or through e-mail, that just that simple step, "walking around being grateful," has made a difference in their lives, and that they are much happier.

Every time that I hear or read those words, I get a great sense of satisfaction and peace and harmony. When I hear from people who I might have helped along a little bit on their road to feeling happy, I feel that I haven't been wasting my time giving people my two cents about the business of happiness.

The best part is, when you choose to focus on gratitude, you'll feel better about everything and you'll even start attracting more positive people in your life. On the other hand, if you focus instead on what you don't have, you'll attract similar people and thoughts, and the cycle of negativity will continue unnecessarily.

One example that I love giving to people when they asked me about happiness, is that if you have a full glass of water and I ask you to fill your glass with milk, you'll have to empty the water and then pour the milk. A very basic concept in physics. Well, I think it works somehow the same with gratitude. If you have your heart full of negativity, bad thoughts, resentments, or sadness, you can't fill your heart with gratitude, first try to "empty" those thoughts from your mind and then you'll have room to start filling it with gratitude. Perhaps a simplistic concept, but I think it makes sense. Pretty soon, the idea of being grateful, will start growing in your heart and soul.

I wish that there was a way to reach these negative people, all of them. I suppose this book can help, and I hope it does, but I know that there will always be people who waste their lives away being sad. But I know, and I'm grateful, that I'm not the only one out there who's trying to spread good ideas about how to be happy. Some time ago, I read a couple of short obituaries in the *Los Angeles Times**. They shared two very interesting and uplifting life stories.

One was about a lady from Japan named Kamato Hongo. She died at the age of 116 — at the time of her death, she was the world's oldest person. To think that the year before she was born, the inimitable pianist and composer Franz Liszt was still alive! In an interview for Japanese TV, they asked her what her secret to health and longevity was, and she said, "An optimistic attitude and not moping around." It's so simple, but I think there's a lot of truth in that. I have learned by talking to many people and through my own personal experiences that an optimistic attitude is essential to being happy.

The second obituary I saw, on that very same day, was about a man named Bob Smith. He owned a TV and radio station in Santa Barbara, California. He was 59 years old when he died. When he had been diagnosed with cancer four years earlier, he said in an interview with Oprah Winfrey that appeared in her magazine: "There are no guarantees in life. But I was given an opportunity to know that an end to my life was coming sooner rather than later. Every sunset becomes more beautiful. Every day with your children becomes more fulfilling. It is a chance to magnify and live 100 hours in one hour, 100 weeks in a few weeks."

What else could anyone say after that? In my opinion, these two stories offer wonderful lessons about life, gratitude, and happiness.

* Los Angeles Times November 2003

CHAPTER III

Love and Family

One of the many things that have contributed to my happiness is that, in the family department, I got lucky. Very lucky.

If you had a great childhood, you probably are happier than most people around you. I know I am. I am one of the luckiest persons in the world, and I had a wonderful childhood. The lessons that I learned during my early years on this planet, given to me mostly by my parents and grandparents, are still vivid and present almost daily in my life. If you did not have a great childhood, my heart goes out to you, because I cannot imagine the alternative.

The very first thing we are exposed to as children is *love*. And it's a good thing too: I think in most cases, the more love you had as a child, the happier you are. After talking to probably thousands of people about this subject, I have come to the (I'm sure not new) conclusion that the happiest people had, as a rule, a very good childhood. I often say that if you can reach back into your memories and recapture the warm, happy moments, the emotions, lessons, and wonders from your childhood, you can continually give yourself some of the greatest gifts in the world.

Such is the case for me. I know that I was extremely lucky. My maternal grandmother was my first piano teacher. Even though my mother used to teach piano, my grandmother became my first teacher for reasons that I truly don't remember. She was a very patient and kind woman with a great love for the piano. I still can see her playing the song "Dark Eyes," an old Russian song that she loved, and Chopin. She would play whatever she was in the mood for. She suffered from arthritis and her fingers were, I remember, somehow crooked. I don't have recollections of her ever complaining about it.

Sometimes her lessons came to me in the form of colloquial expressions. One day, I was playing for some visitors at our house. Well, I suppose some of them were probably not too impressed with my Chopin, and so they started talking while I was performing. After they left, my grandmother said to me, "*La miel no se hizo para la boca del asno.*" The rough translation: "Honey is not meant for a donkey's mouth." Every time I have a rowdy crowd close to my piano, I remember my grandmother and smile about that memory. It helps me continue to enjoy my playing.

I also remember how my grandfather was a great fan of my music. He used to take me all around town, where he was very well known, and introduce me as "Chopincito," or little Chopin. And my mother was always encouraging my dreams of being a pianist and never, ever stopped believing in my talents.

My father, buttressed by his being intensely autodidactic, was a highly cultured man. He had a passion for books that he instilled in all of us. This love for books is, I think, one of the biggest reasons that I am a happy person. My mother used to call my father Don Quixote because, according to her, he was like a knight in a shining armor trying to correct the wrongs of the world and fighting injustice wherever he found it. He was a philosopher and a great storyteller, and our friends were always coming to our house to listen to him. We all learned form his patience. He always thought that to feel happy, you had to have patience. I can still hear him saying, as he often said to us, "Patience is a virtue."

Believe it or not, I never saw my parents fighting or screaming like you see in the movies, or perhaps for some of you, sadly, in real life. Little did I know that a lot of people are not so lucky. But if you *are* one of the lucky ones who had a good childhood, I encourage you to go back in your memories and bring those moments to your present reality. It will make you feel happy all over again.

One of my favorite axioms was written by Oliver Wendell Holmes, the great American legal scholar: "Love is the master key that opens the gates of happiness." Try to always give love and you'll get it back in spades. And a friend of mine from Sweden told me a few years ago an old saying: "If you give bread to life, it comes back to you with butter." I always liked that one too.

You can go down the road to happiness by giving love as much as you can. You'll find that your reserves are unlimited and the results will be quite pleasant in more ways than you can imagine. If you didn't have a great childhood or if you are not close with your family, make a "family" of the friends in your life. Your family may include more than your blood relations; sometimes you have friends that can be just as close, or even closer. Your family consists of the people who take care of you. Anybody that nurtures your soul and gives wings to your dreams is family. That person loves you. Let them into your heart.

A few years ago, a lady that I was dating asked me for my definition of love. I said to her what I still express today: To love someone is to help them become the best that they can be. Find that person. Surround yourself with those kinds of people. You'll see: happiness will be knocking at your door. Give love to life and who knows what'll happen? Maybe some happiness will come your way.

CHAPTER IV

Inconveniences

*Don't let the little inconveniences of
life destroy your inner peace.*

In the overall scheme of life, unexpected problems happen. That's just the way it is. I see these situations in two lights: as little inconveniences or big problems. The ability to distinguish the difference between a little inconvenience and a big problem is stronger in some than in others. It's all about individual perspective. In my life, I've learned to do this pretty well.

I think that one of the many obstacles on the road to happiness, especially in the 21st century, is the tremendous amount of stress that permeates our lives. To live 100% stress-free would be great, but it's impossible, so I think the best thing to do is to take little steps to make life *less* stressful. These steps not only might add years to your life, but also life to your years.

I'll give you a couple of examples of what I mean.

The first thing that comes to mind is traffic — probably because I live in L.A. With eighteen million people living here in the Los Angeles Metropolitan Area and about eight million cars and trucks (DMV statistics for 2016) on the roads, you can deduce that traffic is a stressful part of our daily lives. Unfortunately, traffic congestion is a reality in all of the big cities in the world today and there's not much you or I can do about it.

While driving around in my car with friends, traffic eventually becomes the subject of conversation. You just can't avoid talking about it, not in L.A., because the problem is so obvious and right in your face. People in my car often comment on how I don't get annoyed by the horrible traffic. Sometimes this sentiment is even followed by spontaneous yelling to other cars from the passenger side, where they are seated. When they've calmed down a bit and have caught their breath, they sometimes ask, "OK, Antonio, you really don't look upset; how in the world can do you handle this so well?"

We can keep our fingers crossed until flying cars appear, but in the meantime, there is something better you can do that I think works pretty well. It's worked for me for years, and I've also received some positive feedback about it from friends.

The answer is pretty simple. First of all, when I'm stuck in traffic, I'm consciously reminded right away that I am very lucky to have a car. When I was a child, I remember that, in my hometown Veracruz, only a few lucky people had enough money to own a car. As a child, the idea of owning a car seemed like quite an impossible dream. So, as I sit in traffic, even the worst kind, those thoughts return to me right away. And I think: *I own a car! Not everyone is so lucky.*

Next, I usually think that by virtue of driving that car, even when I'm stuck in terrible traffic, it sure beats walking in the heat, cold, or rain. Where you live, maybe you could add snow to that list. Right away that thought makes me happy, to realize that I have a comfortable car.

But really, there are plenty of more ways to stay positive while you're stuck in traffic. Besides gratitude, think of all the ways you can use that time to yourself, or the conversations you can have when you're in the car with others.

When I'm stuck in bad traffic, I still have all of my philosophical thoughts. I can think about my goals, or even rethink those goals. I can listen to my favorite music. I can listen to my favorite talk shows. Sometimes I even call in to the programs and engage with the hosts or callers, in an effort to bring my point of view about the topic of the moment to the table. Sometimes I'll get some creative ideas in my head; that's why I usually have a tape recorder with me, even in the car. My mind is always racing, thinking about music, books, or new projects. Bad traffic gives me the opportunity to engage my ideas in a positive manner.

The opposite would be to channel that energy and yell and scream at the other cars. That would get nothing accomplished. There would be zero positive effects, and it would probably even annoy the other drivers, not to mention potentially create a confrontation. Remember, when all is said and done, nothing that you do or say in your car will change the speed of the other cars or alleviate the traffic jam you're in. So why waste your time being negative when you could be being productive?

By the time I finish listening to my favorite radio shows or pieces of music, voilà! I have arrived at my destination, and I didn't let the bad traffic ruin my day or my sense of harmony. In fact, my stress levels usually go down, meaning I helped my health and overall well-being. I love to drive!

Next time you're stuck in gridlock, give these suggestions a try. You might find that it's not so bad after all if you just learn to use your time wisely. With this small change in outlook, you'll feel the difference. Little by little, you'll start approaching these situations with a more positive and grateful point of view. Remember, you can either look at these types of things as little inconveniences or big problems. In the grand scheme of things, is something like traffic really such a big deal?

The same can be said for when you're stuck waiting in line, like at the bank, for example. All of us have been stuck at one time or another waiting in line at the bank. I have observed over and over that people waiting in that line often look stressed, anxious, and impatient. It kind of reminds me of the old cowboy movies, where all the cows are in line waiting to go to either the corral or to their final destination.

Don't get me wrong, I'm never exactly happy to be waiting in line either. I would prefer to be playing my piano or composing. But many years ago, I found a way to cope with this little inconvenience. One day I decided to bring a book to the bank. All of a sudden, I found that waiting in line became an almost-pleasant experience. Now whenever I go to the bank, which I rarely do now, I have a book with me.

Many times, especially when I wave at the tellers or other employees at the bank, people comment on the fact that I don't seem to be annoyed by the wait. I always say, "I'm not annoyed; I am reading my book and the time flies." Reading is one of my favorite things.

Sometimes, I'll bring my notes of things to do, or I write down some ideas about my music and shows. In other words, I don't waste the time in line complaining about how long it will take to make it to the teller. It accomplishes nothing and annoys the people around you. I also try to think how lucky I am to have a check or cash to deposit.

I wish more people would think this way. Quite often the person in front of me, especially on Mondays when the lines are longer, will start to fidget around and mutter to themselves about the "lousy service" or the "million things" they have to be doing. I see the looks on their faces and I get the feeling that they're going to go postal at any second. That's why I like to stay positive: it keeps me sane!

As always, whenever you have a positive attitude, you'll find some little extra rewards. Occasionally, while waiting in line, a teller will wave at me, even when one person is in front of me, and they'll say to the waiting crowd, "He has special business that I know how to handle," or something like that. This never makes the person in front of me very happy, but usually, by some universal justice, it happens to the person that has complained the loudest. I can't help but smile inside when that happens.

Also, I always make a point to acknowledge the person behind the window at the bank, either by asking their name, or how they are doing (and meaning it), or by making, in the presence of a female teller, some kind of nice comment about her appearance. That just comes naturally for me. I feel that a kind word, as often as possible, makes that person feel better and I truly believe in the snowballing effect of kindness to strangers.

I remember one time while I was waiting my turn at the bank, I happened to look at the face of one of the tellers and she really looked tired and upset. I guess the previous customer didn't go to charm school and he was not easy to handle. I could tell she was sad from my place in line. When it was finally my turn, I asked her how her day was going, and she gave me the usual "fine, thank you." But her eyes were telling a different story. When she looked at my deposit slip and check, she asked me, "Straight deposit?" and I couldn't help answering, "I've never heard of a gay deposit." She laughed a great laugh and her face finally started to look happy again. We finished the transaction and we said a cheery good-bye. Another time, I told a different teller that they should have a new slogan for the bank: "Join our bank, read a book." She laughed but I don't think she told her manager. By the way, nowadays, I do almost all my banking from my cell phone, so I don't have to go and wait in line anymore!

But really, I am just giving you one small example. This concept can extend to all parts of your life. Throughout the years, I have been rewarded many times over by just small gestures of niceness towards people that I don't know. Just a little humor can make a difference in the way the rest of the day is going for somebody else — and for you. It's not that hard. A bit of caring can go a very long way.

I use these same tactics while standing in line at the post office. I'm pleasant to everybody, and I bring a book. You'd be surprised by how many people tell me, "What a great idea; next time, I'll try that." I think they'll discover the same thing that I did long ago: If you bring a book to the post office, time seems to move faster *and* you'll catch up with your reading. A long wait can then be seen for what it truly is: just a little inconvenience. Why would anybody want to be someone who felt that a long line at the bank or post office was a big problem? Try it my way. Not only will you cut back on stress, but you'll also enrich your mind by reading more books.

A little inconvenience is to discover that you had a flat tire. A big problem is to learn that somebody stole your car. There is a difference.

CHAPTER V

Perspective

Everything is relative. Whenever you think that things aren't going your way, all you have to do is put everything in its proper perspective.

My father used to recite a small poem in Spanish all the time. I don't remember it word for word, but I never forgot its meaning. In a nutshell, it tells the story of a very wise and highly educated man who is broke. In the poem, the man is taking a walk in the park, lamenting his misfortunes in life and wondering out loud. He says something like, "Why don't I have enough money? I am very smart, I work hard, I read and write books, and I am very well educated, yet today all I have to eat is this lousy orange." While walking, he is peeling his orange and throwing away the skin. Soon he realizes that someone has been walking behind him. When he turns around to see who it is, he recognizes one of his colleagues, a man who is at least as intelligent, hardworking, and educated as he is. His friend had been picking up the orange peels that he had been throwing away, and he was eating them. At this point, my father would tell us, "Don't feel sorry for yourself. Remember, there is always someone in worse shape than you. All you have to do is look around and you'll see what I mean."

I think the moral of the story is that when we think we don't have enough or when life is dealing us a bad hand, all we have to do is take the time to look around and observe. If you put it in the proper perspective, you'll probably see that it's not as bad as you initially thought. Of course, you shouldn't take pleasure from somebody else's misfortunes. It's just that they might help you realize that you don't have it so bad. This can be a reassuring thought in your head. It works for me, every single time.

A few years ago, I had an opportunity to put these ideas into practice. Heavy construction work was being done in our condominium. The owners approved the changes knowing that it would take time and money, and that it would be noisy — very noisy.

As a concert pianist, I am used to performing at night. Usually, when I come home from performing, I still have plenty of energy left over from the excitement of playing and entertaining people. That feeling doesn't go away for a while, and so I am pretty excited those nights, even after I'm back in my home. Therefore, only after checking my e-mails, doing some errands in the house, reading, or planning future projects do I finally make it to bed. Late, very late.

Can you imagine my irritation when I was woken up one day at around 7:30 in the morning by the sounds of construction? To me, a musician, that godforsaken hour is better suited for nuns, paperboys, milkmen, and farmers!

The workers were carrying the loads from fixing the swimming pool deck. We lived on the third floor, and the back alley they were using was right under our bedroom. My first thought was to be annoyed at the noise. I don't sleep much as it is, so cutting down my usual pattern to only about four hours was not my cup of milk (I don't like tea).

Then, as always, I put the situation in perspective. I realized that of course it made sense that they would be up and at it so early. It was May in Los Angeles, a time when it's beginning to get hotter during the daytime. Starting work earlier when it is relatively cooler outside makes perfect sense.

I walked to my window and I saw the workers carrying the wheelbarrows filled with rocks and cement up a small ramp to dump them into a large container, which would be carried away at a later date. In other words, these men were up early doing some very hard work, and soon the hot sun would be beating down on their heads. I was trying to imagine the tiredness of their arms and hands and their backs, and the sweat running down their faces, while they were carrying those heavy loads forth and back, forth and back. * Right after that, I knew I needed to stop whining. After all, my job is to put on a nice tuxedo or comfortable suit and play the piano!

A couple of days later, we were dog-sitting for my son and daughter-in-law. I continued to be woken up by the construction noise, so I would take the dog out when this happened. Standing outside, I couldn't help noticing that the workers were speaking in Spanish and they were talking about life, what they were going to do after work or during the coming weekend. When I went back inside, I was walking behind a guy pushing the wheelbarrow. He was whistling and singing quietly to himself. He was happy. I thought to myself that I could probably learn a great deal from him, from his perspective on life. It can be kind of daunting sometimes: the more I read or observe human behavior, the more I realize how much I still have to learn. Other people's perspectives are always valuable. By the way, a couple of years ago I sold the condominium and now I own a house.

Many years ago, I read a story that I never forgot, even though I don't know if it's true. I think that the story took place at a university in the eastern United States. The main characters of the story are two students who are friends and roommates. One semester, they did a lot of partying, and when the grades came out, they discovered that they had received all D's and F's.

They were attending a very expensive private university, so they started to try to figure out how to tell their parents. One student told his friend, "I have to just do it. I am going to call my parents and get it over with." So, he did just that. He called his parents and said, "Hi, Mom and Dad. I'm sorry to tell you this, but at the end of this semester I only got D's and F's." After a long pause, the boy hung up the phone. His friend asked him, "What happened? Tell me." The boy replied, "I'm grounded for the next semester, I can't use the car, I can't go home, and they will pay directly to the school so I can have my meals, but I won't have any extra money. My parents are going to wait until the next semester and then reevaluate my situation. If I get great grades, some of the punishment will be lifted."

Well, the friend didn't like the sound of that. He started to think that just calling his parents would probably not be a good idea, so he wrote them a letter instead, which I will paraphrase here:

Dear Mom and Dad,

How are you? I hope that everybody is fine over there. I have some news, so let me tell you about it right away. Dad, you know how you always tell me that school is very expensive, so I should use my time wisely? Well, you won't have to worry about the financial strain. I am not at the university anymore.

You see, I met this girl and we started dating and she got pregnant. Right away I knew I had to do the right thing and so I asked her to marry me. You're going to be very young grandparents! Isn't that great? We're making plans to get married now, but we have to wait because she's not divorced yet. Her husband is now in jail. It's nothing big, she says, but he has a bad temper. She is such a sweet girl and she has a great mom. Actually, we're staying in her mom's living room to save money. Don't worry about money because I got a job in a hamburger place close to school and my boss says that I could be an assistant manager in a few years, so things are looking up.

Also, remember my car and how you told me the insurance that you pay is very high? Well, you won't have to worry about it anymore. I had a little accident and the car is completely gone. The hospital bill isn't too bad, and they gave me a 40-year plan to pay for it, with a very low interest rate. Isn't that nice? By the way, they found that I have some kind of VD. I have no idea how it happened because Rhonda, my fiancée (and soon to be your daughter-in-law!), seems like a very nice girl. Please don't worry; the doctor says that with a few years of therapy, I'll be able to play sports again, so things are not as bad as they might look now.

Your loving son,

Dirk

PS: Turn the page over, there's more.

On the next page, crafty Dirk wrote:

OK, now that you're getting over the shock, let me tell you the truth. I'm still at the university; I don't have a pregnant girlfriend; I don't even have a girlfriend; I am still living at the dorm at the school; I don't work in any hamburger place; my car is fine; there was no accident; I didn't go to the hospital; and I don't have a VD. None of it was true. However, unfortunately, I got all D's and F's this semester, but I am healthy and I can't wait to go home and be with all of you, play with the dog, and play checkers with Grandma.

Your loving son,

Dirk

A couple of days later, Dirk's parents called. "Are you OK, are you sick? Are you sure there's really no pregnant girlfriend?" And Dirk kept saying, "No, Mom, no." Finally, his mother said, "So really the only truth in your letter is that you got D's and F's?" He insisted that that was all, and she exclaimed, "Thank God! Your Dad and I were worried sick after reading the first page of your letter. Please don't pull that kind of joke on us again. We are really happy that you are OK and we can't wait to see you, but you have to promise to study harder next semester." Of course, Dirk made the promise. His roommate couldn't believe it.

Whether or not this story is true, I find it funny. The extent that some people go to put a different perspective on a situation is just too much for me. But the kid made his point. By taking the time and effort to bring some kind of perspective to his parents, Dirk, as much as most of you might think that he was wrong, accomplished his goal. If he keeps his promise and rededicates himself at school, the bad grades won't be such a big deal after all. It's all about perspective.

Let me make a final point about perspective. I enjoy going to the movies. Since I was a little boy, movie theaters have been wonderful places to temporarily escape and dive into a world of adventure, mystery, comedy, laughter, and new lands. I am and have always been a great movie fan. I enjoy the whole experience: the smell of the popcorn, the ambience of the theater, the anticipation I feel when the previews come on. Unfortunately, my recent movie experiences have been too often diminished by technology. Not by the newest computer graphics, but by cell phones. But I'll talk more about that subject in my next chapter.

Maybe I have a "simplistic mind when it comes to movies," as a lady friend told me a long time ago after we went to see a movie together. At the end of it, she asked me how I liked it and I told her that I had a great time. She gave me this bewildered look like I was crazy, and she told me that it was a terrible movie. Maybe she was right, but a long time ago I decided to enjoy more and criticize less. I am not a movie critic or a movie producer; therefore, I have the luxury of enjoying even movies that the critics hate. I manage to enjoy the music or the photography or whatever aspects I find pleasant in the movie.

I'm glad that I'm not a movie expert and that I'm ignorant of the technical details of moviemaking. I have a friend that studied film in school and I think that he is miserable every time that he goes to the movies because he always finds something wrong. One night I thought I had him cornered. I asked, "Do you like *Casablanca*?" Of course, *Casablanca* is one of the greatest films of all time, a true classic. He answered yes, that he did like it. I started to smile and congratulate him, but then he added: "But…" and went on and on talking about some aspects of the film that he perceived as being wrong.

I think that you can enjoy life more and be happier if, when you walk in a garden, for instance, you focus on the flowers instead of on the leaves that have to be raked. It takes the same time and effort and it makes you feel happier.

So, remember to put life situations in their proper perspective. Everything is truly relative. That correct perspective will help you in your quest for happiness.

* Once in a while you may notice certain peculiar expressions that I use in English. It all goes back to when I came to the U.S. and I was living in Tucson, Arizona. A girl that I was dating, a student at the University of Arizona, advised me that maybe taking English in a program called CESL — Center for English as a Second Language — would help me answer some of the never-ending questions I had about my new language, which I was always pestering friends and acquaintances about. Well, I joined the program and I am sure I drove the teacher crazy.

One day, we were going to take a field trip. In the parking lot, the teacher said to us, "The shuttle goes back and forth from here."

I said to her, "I think it is forth and back. First you go forth and then you come back, so it's forth and back, not back and forth."

She laughed and commented, "You probably have a point, but it's back and forth!"

What a funny language!

CHAPTER VI
Cell Phones

If you love your cell phone more than anything else in the world, you really need to read this chapter.

I love some technology. I'm writing this book on my computer, and that makes my life so much easier. After playing the piano for hours, writing by hand would be a bit hard for me. Still, every coin has two sides.

When cell phones first came out a few years ago, I was one of the first to get one. The two main reasons were 1) my son would be able to find me anytime and I could be there for him for whatever reason, and 2) driving home late from my job playing the piano was always a bit risky. I was playing at the beautiful L'Orangerie restaurant, one of the most elegant dining places in the U.S. To go home to Sherman Oaks, I had to take Coldwater Canyon from Beverly Hills. If I ever got a flat tire going through that canyon, I'd be in trouble, because there is nothing but houses and there are no public telephones on the road. The cell phone became a good friend in times of need.

Now fast-forward to the present. Not too long ago, I was sitting at the Music Center in Los Angeles, watching the opera *La Boheme*, and I heard a cell phone ring. I found that very, very rude; I call it a mood breaker at best.

It's gotten so ridiculous that before operas, recitals, plays, concerts, and even church congregations, there is now the ever-present announcement to "please turn off your cell phones, Blackberries and pagers." By the way, who carries pagers today?

Last year, I was playing the piano at a funeral service for an acquaintance of mine, and in the middle of the sermon a cell phone started ringing. I give you my word, it happened twice.

Personally, the pleasure of going to the movies has been diminished by the ringing of cell phones in the movie house. I don't think that any of the calls are for emergency open heart surgery, either. As you can see, this issue bothers me. In fact, it is one aspect of my business of happiness that I'm still trying to learn and cope with to this day. But I'm working on it.

Let me tell you about another phenomenon I often witness these days while watching people from my piano bench. At the present time, I am the resident pianist at the world-famous Peninsula Hotel in Beverly Hills. The Peninsula is truly an oasis of beauty and elegance. The Living Room where I play is a gorgeous place with fine very comfortable and elegant couches and there's always a fire crackling in the fireplaces, all year round. Almost every night I observe with never-ending curiosity a group of two or three men or women or couples talking on their cell phones but *not to each other*. Am I the only one that thinks something's wrong with this picture?

I always thought that going out with friends to have a drink or a bite or to listen to music was supposed to be a social event. At least that's the way it's been for the last couple thousand years, I'm pretty sure. I have witnessed couples that only talk to friends on the cell phone. I have seen people very, very annoyed and upset by the sounds of cell phones ringing in a horrible cacophony of noise that does not belong in these places. I have seen (especially among the teenage and twenty-something crowd) people sliding their fingers over their screens over and over, as if they're waiting for a miracle to happen, opening and closing their cell phones in a constant race with no winners or goals.

I think that cell phones are like a drug to which people are getting more and more addicted. When you go to the bank or the post office and you don't even stop for a few seconds to acknowledge the person behind the counter because you're just too busy on your cell phone, well, I think that there must be something wrong with your manners.

Luckily, every once in a while, I do get some welcome relief. A couple of years ago, I was standing in line at a post office in downtown Los Angeles. A guy who was talking (very loudly, as these types usually do) on his cell phone approached the counter and just handed a couple of letters to the postal attendant, without saying a word to her. To the rest of the customers' pleasant surprise, the lady attendant said to him in a firm voice, "When you are finished with your call, I'll take care of you. Next!" We felt like applauding! The rude man quickly finished his call and went back to the counter.

I understand that technology is great and that cell phones provide a new level of communication. I just think that there is a courteous and proper way to use them. Using them correctly, with other people in mind, can help you contribute to the happiness of others instead of being a constant irritator. It's simple: if you're at the opera, the movies, or church, *turn off your cell phone!* No one else wants to hear it, believe me. I know that it might be some kind of a sacrifice for some of you, but try it, for everyone else's sake around you. Trust me, you'll live!

One day while I was waiting in line to get my ice-blended green tea (a new drink that I love, in addition to ice-blended mochas), I struck up a conversation with a young lady in front of me — that is, when she finally closed her cell phone. I asked her, "What would you do without your cell phone for one day?" She looked at me like I was Count Dracula. With that look of horror and disbelief on her face, she told me, "I would die without my phone!" I don't think she was kidding.

Overall, I am very glad that I have a cell phone. It has been a help more than once, but it is still where it belongs, in my car, in the "glove compartment." (In all my years in the United States, I have never met a single person who keeps his or her gloves in the glove compartment! Why do they call it that?). Actually, a correction now, I don't keep my cell phone there anymore. It's in the cup holder.

I have witnessed at the Hotel young couples texting non-stop. One time I asked one couple who were they texting non-stop and they told me "we're texting each other". Can you believe it? The other night I arrived at the hotel and I saw in the Living Room about 18 young ladies finishing their afternoon tea, while I was opening my piano, I noticed that 17 of them were on their cell phones!

I see people crossing the streets not looking at the traffic, only their cell phones. That's amazing to me. AAA reports that cell phone use and teens are a bad combination while driving, "even worse than we thought". This is a direct quote from the National Safety Council: "reports that cell phone use while driving leads to 1.6 million crashes every year. 1 out of 4 car accidents in the US is cause by texting or calling and driving. According to the National Highway Traffic Safety Administration, in 2017, 3,166 persons were killed by distracted driving. If this statistic doesn't scare you in to being more careful with the use of your cell phone in the car or walking on the streets, nothing will. When I make a call in my car, I don't hold the cell on my hand, it's all done while I keep my hands on the steering wheel.

We are seeing more and more videos of people getting hurt, sometimes badly, walking in the streets or malls while watching their cell phone screens non-stop. Quite often when I go to the restroom at the hotel or at restaurants, I witness men going about their business while holding their phones with one hand!

Please, be discreet with your cell phone. You'll make everyone around you happier, and maybe you'll learn something by talking to the people you're with for a change.

CHAPTER VII

"Here Comes Santa Claus"

*The road to happiness has many
interesting detours.*

I think it is up to everyone to find, embrace, and explore some of the detours that life puts in front of us all from time to time, even though many choose not to. These small challenges can sometimes bring big rewards.

A few years ago, during the Christmas season while I was still playing at Macy's Plaza in downtown Los Angeles, something very interesting happened to me. I was playing some Christmas carols and the line to see Santa Claus was getting longer and longer, although there was no sign of Santa in the mall. The photographer came over and asked me if I knew anything about it, and some parents also came to my piano to ask me the same question. I looked at my watch and I realized that Santa was 20 minutes late. I wasn't sure what to do, so I closed the piano and went upstairs to the management office — the place where I was hired and also where Santa would go to change clothes.

I asked the concierge in charge and she told me in a worried voice, "Santa just called. He was in a small car accident and he's OK, but he won't be able to make it today and I just called the agency and it's too late for them to send another Santa. I guess I'm going to go downstairs and tell the crowd about it." I couldn't help remembering the look of happiness that my own son had every Christmas season when he would first see Santa in the mall; his face would light up with joy and his head became filled with dreams of toys, presents, and candy. Immediately I said to her, "I know you have a Santa outfit here, so if you want me to, I'll change right away and go downstairs, and I'll be Santa." She thought about it for a second, then smiled and said, "Why not, Antonio?" So, I did. I put the Santa outfit on and before I got to the elevator carrying a small basket of candy canes, I was already sweating due to the large, bushy white beard and felt-lined red hat. I made it downstairs with plenty of "HO-HO-HOs" along the way and sat in the Santa chair.

After I sat down in the official Santa chair and saw the faces of the children and grown-ups waving at me, you could not imagine the joy and sense of happiness that I had. For two and a half hours I lived a fantasy of make-believe. I listened to fanciful stories and answered the questions of wide-eyed admirers to the best of my ability. I wondered later what the children thought about my accent. After all, I don't think that many people imagine Santa Claus with a Mexican accent. But, surprise, surprise — nobody mentioned it. Also, having some pretty young ladies sitting on my lap was an added bonus to the already joyous occasion.

Then something funny happened just before the end of my Santa gig. Well, funny for me, anyway. Looking at the children in line, I couldn't help noticing a brother and sister. I assumed they were siblings. The parents were busy talking to the photographer and getting their own camera ready. The boy, older and taller than his sister, was pushing and shoving the little girl out of his way. I noticed that when they walked to get in line (she was wearing a lovely dress), she reached the end of the line first. He came after her and pushed her out of the way. Obviously surpassing her in strength, this did not prove to be a difficult task for him. Shortly afterwards, he actually wanted her out of the line altogether. The little girl had no help from anybody. It probably wasn't a big deal, just kids being kids, but it didn't sit well with me.

When their turn finally came, the boy sat on my lap and started telling me all the toys that he wanted. I listened patiently and when he finished, he asked me, "I know that you are not Santa, you are probably one of his helpers, but do you think that he is going to get me my presents?" I waited a few seconds and with a serious look I said, "Probably...*not*." You should have seen the surprised look on his face! He asked me, "What? Why not?" I replied, "The little girl waiting in line is your sister, right?" He said yes. "I have been watching how you pushed her and didn't want her to be in line...." He immediately changed the tone of his voice and tried to come up with some excuses. I said to him, "I don't think that Santa likes boys that push little girls. You should protect your sister. She probably admires you and looks up to you for protection, don't you think so?" He nodded and when I noticed that the message was beginning to get through, I said, "I'll make you a deal: You promise to be nice and gentle to your sister and I'll talk to Santa about your toys." He beamed a smile from ear to ear and emphatically promised, "OK!"

After I spoke with his sister and decided to stand and stretch a bit, I looked for that family. They were walking away towards one of the stores, the parents slightly ahead of the children. The boy was holding his little sister's hand. I waved at them and they waved back, a big smile on their faces, and on mine.

My Santa experience was unforgettable. I now appreciate even more how hard it is to do that job. It gave me a different kind of happiness and I hope that I was able to share some of it with the people who came to my chair.

Growing up in Veracruz, Mexico, we didn't have malls or Santas, so when I came to the States and discovered the malls, all dressed up in their Christmas decorations, my first Santa sighting was, as silly as it may sound to some of you, a wonderful wonderland of dreams, joys, and happiness. I think that watching my own son being so happy about it became contagious to me and every year, with a Pavlovian kind of effect, I get the same feelings of happiness and joy when I hear the first songs of the season or come across the smell of warm Christmas cookies.

Once in a while life puts new paths in front of you. It's up to you to take them or not. I like to explore those new directions. Sometimes, happy moments are around the corner. Take a chance, explore another detour. A boat is safe and sound when it's docked in the harbor, but I think that boats are meant to sail.

CHAPTER VIII

Don't Rain on My Parade

*I don't like the idea of trampling
on the happiness of others.*

Many years ago, a young lady who was a piano student of mine told me that her mother was very strict and always corrected her manners when she was a girl. There's nothing wrong with disciplining children, of course, but in this case, I think the mother took it to the extreme. The young lady told me that one day she finally came home with straight A's on her report card. She ran into the house crying, "Mom, Mom, I have my report card! Straight A's!" She still remembers the answer from her mother: "I told you not to slam the door!" Even all those years later, that painful memory was still engraved in the young lady's thoughts.

I think that there is a time and a place to correct or criticize other people's opinions or behaviors. I feel happy about the fact that I really don't like to rain on other people's parades. But not everyone has a problem doing just that.

Sometimes, when I am playing, a customer requests a song, let's say "Embraceable You," by Gershwin, one of my favorites. It happened not too long ago. A lady asked for the song and another person sitting next to her said to both of us, "I really don't like that song."

Of course, I still played the song. A guest made a request and I always comply if I can. The point is that *nothing* was gained by her comment, especially since the two were enjoying drinks and food together. I could see in the face of the lady who requested the song a look of quiet disappointment. Don't you think that it's easier to share somebody else's happiness, even if whatever they might enjoy is not your cup of "milk"?

Sometimes, friends or acquaintances tell me: "I loved that movie." Whatever that movie might be, if I also liked it, I'll share the experience. But if the movie was not to my liking, what in the world could I gain by raining on their happiness? There is nothing that you can do about it. They cannot "un-see" the movie, so leave them alone and let them enjoy their happy moment.

Just by allowing the people around you to express their ideas and feelings without putting them down, especially if it's already a done deal anyway, you can greatly contribute to their sense of happiness.

My two cents of advice on the subject? If people around you put you down about your taste in clothing, movies, music, or books, stay away from them. Life is too short to hang around negative and pessimistic people. Remember, you have the choice to stay away from them. Exercise that choice.

Now if you ask me my opinion about a subject, I will tell you my (usually very strong) ideas without reservations. But I'll never say something to purposefully take joy away from someone else.

Believe me, it's not that hard. It is true, however, that moments of joy sometimes trigger a certain degree of envy in others. Life has taught me that. So, try to put a little effort into not raining on anybody's parade. You'll both feel better, I promise.

CHAPTER IX

Calisthenics for Your Mind

Magazines, movies, TV, infomercials, radio, newspaper ads — you name it, everywhere you turn, it's all about being attractive and thin.

One of the conditions of L.A. life is being constantly reminded to keep your body in shape. On several occasions, ladies that I have dated asked me to show them my muscles. My answer was and always is, "If I wanted to show you my muscles, I'd have to shave my head."

Unfortunately, nobody tells you to exercise the most important muscle in your body: your mind. I'd like to think one main factor that contributes to my sense of happiness is the fact that I have always enjoyed exercising my brain. Luckily for me, as a pianist and composer, it's something that I do every day. But I also enjoy extracurricular calisthenics for my mind.

I think that the more you exercise your brain, the less time you'll have to feel sorry for yourself, and more good things will happen to you. You might increase your brainpower and perhaps, by default, become happier while you're at it.

I am lucky because I learned to love learning when I was just a little boy. My father used to tell us stories and teach us games to try to solve. Many of the puzzles couldn't be solved by simply looking up the answers in books. Instead, their solutions could usually only be determined by the use of logic, or what somebody called in a book that I read many years ago "lateral thinking."

Let me tell you one of my favorite puzzles. This little puzzle will hopefully illustrate what kind of solutions you can find by simply doing something that is becoming less and less a part of our lives: thinking things through. Because we live very busy and hectic lives, the marvelous moments (for me) of quietly *thinking* are becoming few and far between, and surely less frequent than in my parents' time, when they didn't have the distractions of TV, e-mails, faxes, computers, phones, etc.

But anyway, here is the puzzle. You can find the solution at the end of the book, but give yourself some time to solve it. Don't just cheat and look at the answer right away!

There are three crates in front of you. One is labeled "Apples," the second "Oranges," and the third "Apples and Oranges." *Every crate has an incorrect label.* Your job is to go to *only* one box of your choosing, pick up one piece of fruit without looking inside, and, just by looking at that fruit, put the labels on all of the correct boxes.

This puzzle seems very hard at the beginning, but the solution is quite simple. I'll give you a hint: the answer has nothing to do with smell. You just have your powers of deduction to guide you to the right box, pick up the fruit, and figure out the rest. Good luck!

When I was young, I also used to enjoy reading Sir Arthur Conan Doyle's *Sherlock Holmes* stories, mainly because the solutions to the mysteries could always be found using the deductive process. Reading is one of my greatest pleasures. And it doesn't have to be a mystery story to be good exercise for your brain.

Besides reading and solving logic puzzles, I do something else that I know stimulates my mind: I play chess. I read an interview with a group of nuns that appeared in a national magazine a few years ago — I think it was *LIFE*. The nuns were over 90 years old, still sharp as tacks, and they all played chess. I am sure that there is a connection between that game and the powers of the mind.

There is something marvelous in the way that chess forces you to think. That process, I think, might stimulate some parts of your brain that otherwise may never be moved.

But I would say that by far the best exercise for my mind is music, which opens up pathways in the brain in the most wonderful way. I even used music to help my son increase his learning ability. When he was very, very young, around three years old, I devised a musical game for him. I started by playing Tchaikovsky's *Piano Concerto #1*, and I would repeat the name of the piece to him several times. Eventually I would play different parts of it and then, out of the blue, I would play no more than two or three seconds of that concerto and he always could name it. It became a fun game for us. The game evolved to include many different pieces of music. My son would sometimes get overly anxious and try to guess very fast. Eventually the game evolved to focus on how many seconds it would take for him to name each piece. Sometimes he could do it in only two seconds, believe it or not. Was he a baby genius? I don't think so; I only stimulated his brain in a different fashion. Another musical piece that he loved was Rachmaninoff's *Third Piano Concerto*, and we listened to a live Horowitz recording many times. The other night he mentioned to me that it is still his favorite classical piece.

One time, my son and I were invited to see a Broadway show; I think it was *Me and My Girl*. My friend Laura Waterbury, a singer and actress who performed on Broadway and movies for many years, is the one who took us to the theater. I had told her about my musical games with my son and she was a bit, let's say, curious but skeptical.

As usual, just like every other time that we made plans to go to see musical theater, I bought the soundtrack, and during our rides in the car I would play it over and over until both my son and I became familiar with the music. The day that we went to the theater, my son sat between both of us, and before the music started I whispered to him, "You are going to have to help my friend because she is not familiar with the names of the songs, so please, as soon as the song begins, tell her the name of it." Lo and behold, a couple of seconds into each song in the show, he would whisper the name to my friend and she just couldn't believe it. For years, Laura would still mention that night with a big smile on her face. Sadly, she passed away in 2013.

For children, these types of mental games are just that: games. They don't realize that they are learning and that these puzzles and games can contribute to the growth of their minds. Besides developing their reasoning skills and ability to think of new ideas, I also think puzzles and games contribute to their sense of happiness. In fact, Maria Montessori made a career out of it.

By the way, maybe by accident, who knows, my son developed, while he was in first grade, his own way of doing math by flipping his hands forth and back. He showed it to his teacher and I remember her getting a kick out of it. The following year, his "system" was gone, but the tools he used to create it — the powers of his mind — will always be there.

So, to help you get further along on the road to happiness, or to help you stay happy, I recommend exercising your mind as much as you can. I read a very interesting book on that subject, *The Playful Brain*, by Richard Restak, M.D. The premise is the surprising science of how puzzles improves your mind. Read a book. Play chess. Learn to play a musical instrument. You can do brain calisthenics any time, any place — even, remember, while waiting in the monstrous lines at your local postal office.

CHAPTER X

Not Tonight, Dear...

Walk into an elevator at a mall or where you work and say "Hello, how are you?" to the people inside. Most likely the first words out of their mouths will be, "I am tired."

I truly believe that we are living in the "I'm tired" culture. Growing up, I don't remember my father, grandmother, friends, or teachers being stuck in this exhausted mentality.

Still, I strongly believe that today, saying "I'm tired" is more of a habit and a sense of communion with friends and coworkers than actually speaking the truth. Let me give you a couple of examples.

The other day, I walked into an elevator in a shopping mall close to my house and a couple of ladies were talking. One of them had a little girl who was about two years old. She was in her carriage. I smiled to the child, and she smiled back. She was playing with some toys and quietly singing to herself. She was a picture of happiness and portrayed a sense of living life. To my amazement, the mother said to her friend, "She is very tired now." Her friend nodded in agreement. Then she looked at the little girl and she said, "You're so tired."

The girl was *not* tired. She was anything but tired. She kept singing and playing. But there is no doubt in my mind that after listening to her mother saying to her day after day, "You are tired," the little girl will *feel* tired, whether she truly is or not. We always talk about the power of the mind and once in a while we can testify to the truth of that statement.

Years ago, I was in a band with my brothers in Mexico City. We were ready to go onstage and decided to play a prank on the lead singer from the other band that was just finishing up and getting ready to come off. The lead singer was a guy from Spain, a nice, pleasant guy. My brothers, some of the waiters, and some other musicians, after previously agreeing to "have some fun," decided to tell him, as soon as he came off stage, "Tonino — (I think that was his name) — you look sick, are you OK?" And he would say, "Yes, I'm fine." Then each person said the same thing and he kept answering the same way. One hour later, he was sick! We were not proud of our silly little joke because we saw, firsthand, the incredible power of the mind. He believed what we were telling him, even though it wasn't true at all. It was just a joke, but we regretted it. That was a lesson I never forgot.

As I mentioned before, I played the piano at Macy's Plaza for 11 years. Walking into the office each day, I would hear the constant cries of "I'm so tired!" and everybody agreeing. When they would ask me how I was doing, I would always say, truthfully, "I feel great." I would receive these strange looks and half-smiles, and then they would go back to talking amongst themselves about why they were "so tired."

I knew that by asking the young receptionist (she was in her early 20s), "How are you today?" I would get the usual answer: "I'm so tired!" So, one day I decided to analyze the situation a bit.

It was a Monday morning. I walked into the office and asked the usual questions, "How are you? Did you have a good weekend?" And she answered the usual "I'm sooo tired!" So far, the day was progressing as normal.

After I finished my playing at about 2:00 p.m., I went back into the office and we talked about the weekend in more detail. She asked me about mine and I gave her the rundown. It went something like this: "Friday, after I left here, I ran a few errands, went home, answered some e-mails, read a bit, got dinner, and then I went to the Hotel Bel-Air, where I played from eight to one in the morning. After the hotel, I went home, read some more, wrote a song, and went to sleep. Saturday morning, I played my usual tennis game with Bob, went out for breakfast, read, made some business calls, got dinner, and went to the hotel for the same schedule. Sunday morning, I went to pick up my son, we played tennis, went to see a Dodger game, and had an early dinner. Then I took him to his mother's and I went to pick up my date for the evening. That was my weekend and I feel great being back here Monday morning."

Then it was her turn: "Friday when I finished here, my boyfriend picked me up, we had an early dinner, and he took me home. Saturday morning, I got up late, did some laundry, and then my boyfriend came to pick me up. We went to see a movie and had a late dinner. Sunday morning, I got up even later, hung around the house, watched a couple of movies on TV, had an early dinner, and went right to bed."

I was thinking, how in the world could she say that she is tired? I don't think that the weekend was hard work for her, but nevertheless she said she was tired. After I asked her again, "Are you sure you are tired?" she thought about it and she finally answered, "Actually...not really." I rest my case.

There is a sense of camaraderie about somebody in a group saying "I'm tired" and everybody else agreeing. I never agree, so I always get funny looks. I think that maybe I have brainwashed myself into not being tired, and now I simply take it as fact. But still, it works, I don't feel tired. You can ask anybody that I ever dated, plus my friends and relatives, and they'll tell you the same thing: "I don't know why, but Antonio is never tired." I am not that strong.

I'm not Superman. I just have told myself so many times throughout the years that I didn't feel tired that maybe, just maybe, my brain believes my words.

It works for me; maybe it will work for you. Starting today, say to yourself, over and over, "I'm not tired," like some kind of mantra. When a friend tells you that he or she is tired, first ask why. They might have a really good reason, but the usual answer is something like, "I really don't know, but I'm tired." If that's the case, then probe them a bit more, and ask what they did to merit being tired. They might just realize that they really don't have a reason to feel tired, that it's all in their head.

Unless you have a medical condition, like chronic fatigue, you might discover that saying "I'm tired" is worse than just a habit — it can really wear you down, and for no good reason. Break that habit and you'll be making progress towards feeling more alive and being happier.

CHAPTER XI

Have You Ever Sung a Song on a Public Bus?

I think one of the secrets to being happy is to never lose the ability to see the wonders of the world through the eyes of a child.

I collected baseball cards when I was a boy, for a short period of time. I have also collected stamps, records, books, coins, and photos in my lifetime.

But my favorite collection is not tangible. I can't show it to you in a material sense, although I can share it with as many people as I want. I collect memories. Especially the good ones. My grandmother used to say, "*Recordar es vivir*," which means, "To remember is to live."

Boy, she was right. I have a habit of remembering wonderful and beautiful memories all the way from my childhood in Mexico to the present, right here and now in Los Angeles, California.

I have been accused by some women I have dated in the past of having a selective memory, and they probably have a point. Usually, during disagreements, they would have one recollection of facts and I would have another. Chances are they were right because they had an acute way of remembering details and situations. I had and still have the habit of remembering only the good memories, the good situations, the *happy* moments.

I think it has always been an automatic response in my brain. I always focus and remember the good stuff, and the bad goes right out the window. Maybe that's one of the reasons I consider myself a very happy man. Maybe that's one of the reasons that the stress levels in my life have been as low as can be reasonably imagined. Maybe it has helped me to be a happier human being.

It's no coincidence that I still have friendships with ladies that I dated in the past. Most of them still remain my friends. No hard feelings, no fights, hopefully no bad memories. And, as the years have gone by, it has become easier and easier, I'm happy to say, to always focus on the good moments of the day and push aside all the negative circumstances that all of us are exposed to in our daily lives.

Maybe you could try this little exercise: Every day, try to remember a happy moment from your childhood or your adult life or your school days or your college days, or even from as recently as last week or, if you're lucky, from yesterday or today. Once you get in the habit of always trying to remember happy times, they eventually will permeate more and more of your thoughts and will slowly help you become a happy person. If you already consider yourself happy, maybe this habit will make you even happier.

The next step is creating those happy moments when you can. If you ask me, just because you're getting older doesn't mean you can't play. If I didn't play, I would probably feel much older! George Bernard Shaw said, "We don't stop playing because we grow old; we grow old because we stop playing".

One of the great pleasures of my life is to remember my wonderful childhood. Today, as an adult, I don't want to forget the wondrous beauty of the world through a child's eyes, or my never-ending remembrances of fantasies and dreams.

My two cents of advice are to never lose your sense of wonder. I still get excited about going to the movies, or to a concert or at the thrill of walking into Dodger Stadium, seeing a beautiful rainbow, enjoying a concert by the Los Angeles Philharmonic in Disney Hall, seeing something beautiful around me. Seeing Paris again. Some people play it very cool; nothing makes them go "wow!" I am not like that; I haven't lost my sense of wonder and I know that I will never lose it. Sometimes seeing life through the eyes of a child is another reminder of the beauty that the world offers all of us.

Edna St. Vincent Millay said it better: "Childhood is the kingdom where no one dies." A good way to grab some moments of happiness during a busy day is to find that instant where the child in you takes over, even if it's only for a few minutes or even seconds. In my case, it sometimes happens for a lot longer than that.

Yes, I do pay my bills on time. Yes, I am reliable with my jobs. Yes, I do keep my goals in mind. But if I'm so responsible, how do I capture those silly moments that add happiness to my life and help me build the treasure of memories that I so cherish? Well, I think that sometimes you have to try to make happy moments happen.

Let me tell you a couple of funny stories.

Years ago, when I was still living in Mexico City, I was playing piano professionally and I was also in a band with my brothers. Like the previous story I told you in the last chapter, once in a while we would do something silly. One day after a few hours of rehearsal, one of our friends challenged one of my brothers and me to try something daring, which I guess is sort of an old Mexican "tradition." He said, "I know that you are well known here in Mexico, but I dare you to get on a public bus on Reforma Avenue (a famous avenue in Mexico City) and sing for the passengers." My brother Francisco and I looked at each other and shrugged, "Why not?"

So, my brother grabbed his guitar and off we went to the first bus stop close to our house. Since we were lucky enough to live in a peaceful neighborhood, we weren't too concerned about the treatment from the passengers. We got on the bus, paid our fee, sat down, and my brother started singing and playing his guitar. My brother had a pleasant voice. He sang in pitch. At the end of the song, the passengers applauded and I immediately gave him his first "tip," in the form of a crisp bill.

After I made the appearance of giving him money, he walked up and down the bus collecting real tips. We did that to the amazement of our friend, who was sitting in the bus incognito. We then did it on a few more buses. We came back home with a few extra pesos and laughter to last a lifetime. When I get together with my brothers, it's always a lot of fun to remember those childlike, crazy but harmless days.

On another occasion, I went to Universal Studios with my son. One of the park's shows at the time involved "space-walking" astronauts, and the host asked for a volunteer to come and suit up. My son, jumping up and down, pointed right at me, yelling, "My dad, my dad will do it!" Well, as you can probably guess, the host invited me onstage and proceeded to put the astronaut suit on me. Up I went with some cables along with a couple of other guys, and we pretended that we were in space. I did lots of my silly poses, pretending to shoot the other astronauts, etc. My son had a great time laughing a lot, and I did too. A great moment of happiness was created by the will to just make my child happy. More memories to last a lifetime.

Another time, my son and I were at Dodger Stadium. The music started playing, with a dancing rhythm. I jumped out of my seat and started dancing. Pretty soon, we looked up at the big screen that hung-over left field and guess who was on the big picture? Yep, yours truly. We had a great laugh and even more memories for our personal memory banks.

Speaking of baseball, I'm sure you are familiar with the song everyone sings during the seventh-inning stretch, "Take Me Out to the Ball Game." At another Dodger game one day, while singing that song, I read the lyrics on the big screen a little more carefully than usual. First of all, I asked my son, "What do they mean by 'Take me out to the ball game?' We're already *at* the ball game. And 'Take me out to the park?' We're already *in* the park!" My son gave me that "What are you talking about, Dad?" look, but he got a kick out of it.

On yet another trip to Dodger Stadium, we were singing the aforementioned song, and when we got to the "Buy me some peanuts and Cracker Jacks" line, I did another one of my careful examinations of the English language and said to my son, "I think the lyrics are wrong." He gave me the same "Are you nuts?" look and told me, "Dad, your English is not perfect; they know what they're doing." I proceeded to tell him, "I think that it should be 'Buy me some peanuts and Cracker *Jack*,' not Jacks," and I went and bought the candy and showed him the box. It is written *Cracker Jack*, not *Cracker Jacks*. He still didn't believe that I was right, so the following day I called the Dodgers' office and asked for someone in public relations. I told the gentleman who answered the phone my opinion about Cracker Jack and the song. He answered, "Thank you for your call, we'll look into it. And thank you for supporting the Los Angeles Dodgers."

Guess what happened? A few weeks later we were back at the ballpark and in the seventh inning we stood up to sing the song. Wonder of wonders, the big screen had the lyrics flashing with the music, except that this time it read, "Buy me some peanuts and Cracker *Jack*!" I jumped up and yelled to my son, "Look! They changed the lyrics!" We laughed and laughed and sang a little louder than usual that day.

By the way, what did I get for my contribution to the correct lyrics? A couple of tickets to see a future game? A baseball hat? A thank-you note? Nothing, zip, nada. Not even a lousy hot dog! That's OK though. I had a great laugh, and every time that I go to Dodger Stadium, I smile knowing that I am the reason (in my humble opinion) they changed the lyrics.

So, there you go, yet another silly occasion to be happy about and to add to my happiness memory bank. You get my drift. Sometimes, you have to pursue happy moments; that way all together they will create an inexhaustible collection of happy memories, little by little. Maybe that's another contributing factor towards the goal to happiness. Unusual or out-of-the-ordinary situations can sometimes create moments that will greatly add to your sense of happiness. Sometimes you have to look for and discover those moments yourself. Would you like some more examples?

A few years ago, my son and I went to Cancún, Mexico. It's a beautiful place with the softest sand you'll ever feel under your feet. We did something that not many people get to do: we swam with dolphins. Because of environmental reasons, there are simply not that many places in the world where you can try it. We went to a gorgeous beach called Ixcaret. We got there very early in the morning. We ran from the tour bus to the ticket office, where they had a limited number of tickets for sale, and we did it. Swimming with the dolphins was one of those unforgettable moments in our lives. More deposits in our memory banks. More happy moments to remember.

Another time, because I got to play piano for some sponsors of the Olympic Games in Los Angeles in 1988, I was fortunate enough to be invited to the opening ceremonies. For the closing ceremonies, the invitation was extended also to my son.

At the Olympics, we both had one of those once-in-a-lifetime moments to cherish and remember. To see the most exceptional athletes from all over the world marching, singing, holding hands, and just being filled with joy was an unforgettable experience for everybody at the stadium that day. All the flags and citizens from different countries melted into a great mountain of pure humanity.

Sometimes you have to pursue the happy moments with planning, determination, and a touch of luck. You have to make them happen. You can't let fate be the only factor, although sometimes fate plays a big role.

Which brings me to another story. When the Olympic Games came back to the U.S. in Atlanta in 1996, my son and I reminisced about the '88

Games and thought how fun it would be to go again. Not having enough money to go was not going to stop me from finding alternatives. I founded my chance by listening to the radio.

A local radio station had a promotion in which the winner of a drawing of postcards sent in by listeners would be sent to the Olympics in Atlanta along with a companion. As you have probably ascertained by now, I am an optimist and I have faith, so for many nights I thought about that postcard with dreams of going to the Olympics with my son. I sent my postcard, and guess what happened. Yes! They announced my name on the radio. I called and I was notified as the winner. So once again, my son and I got to go to the Olympics. More happy moments. More happy memories for our memory banks.

I could tell you so many stories about not ever losing the child in my heart. I have danced in a Disneyland parade — wearing a tutu. And I had a wonderful time. Yet again, my son and my girlfriend were laughing like crazy, because Antonio Castillo de la Gala, the accomplished pianist who usually is seen in a suit and tie or a tuxedo, was dancing in a goofy (no pun intended) parade and looking ridiculous. It's moments like those that help build a personal and familial road towards the elusive state of happiness.

So, go ahead. You're *never* too old to play or to be a child at heart. Try letting go, try making these moments happen. The choice is yours. Keep adding to your memory bank. The happier memories you have, the easier it will be to make withdrawals. And the best part is that there's no maximum limit to how many happy memories you can deposit. Try it. Be happy!

CHAPTER XII

Race: Check the Appropriate Box

Another factor that contributes heavily to my
own sense of happiness is the fact that I have
never fallen into the trap of groupthink.

When I came to the United States from Mexico, the first city where I lived was Tucson, Arizona. In the beginning, my life in the States was full of surprises and situations that were foreign to me. A never-ending cornucopia of styles, customs, and cultural changes were appearing in front of my eyes on a daily basis.

One such instance that particularly sticks out in my mind occurred when I filled out a job application for my first engagement in the United States, at the finest restaurant in Tucson. It was called the Tack Room and the owners were a lovely family. After writing down the usual information — name, date of birth, address, etc. — I got to a question that was new to me and that I had never seen before during my life in Mexico: *race*. See, I don't know if it is still true today, but as far as I can recall, nobody was asked that question in Mexico. I called my brothers and I asked friends back home if they ever recalled encountering that question on job applications and the answer was always the same: never.

So, I wrote what to me was the only possible answer in my brain: human. I don't want to sound crazy, but I have always seen myself, and for that matter all people, as members of one race: the human race. That's the only race that matters.

I think that a person's own sense of individuality helps create his or her own sense of value and worth *independently* from any other outside circumstances. And I have always believed that it is foolish to be "proud" of where you were born (you had *nothing* to do with it), the color of your skin (totally irrelevant and again, you had nothing to do with it — unless you tan heavily, I guess), your height, etc. I have always had this sense and belief that my home is the planet earth and "my people" are my fellow human beings.

That seemingly harmless thought has made me unpopular when that subject comes up, especially when I have called talk-radio shows to express my feelings. The sentiments on race in that field are strong, very strong. Whenever I hear people on the radio, in person, or on TV arguing the "pros" of their race, I react with anger and frustration. And let me tell you, you cannot be happy and angry at the same time.

One time, the topic of race was being discussed on a radio station and the guest of the program was a Latino "activist" talking about the pride in *La Raza* (in Spanish, *La Raza* literally means "the race"). Well, I thought what he was saying was foolish, so I called in. When he asked me my race, I said "human." He didn't like my answer.

Let me try to express how I formed this opinion about the race issue, and why I think my view is correct.

I was born in Mexico and now I am an American citizen by choice. My son was born in the United States. My great-grandparents were from Spain, Italy, and France. Recently, I just found that through DNA research, that I also have heritage from England. Don't ask me how, I have no idea, but I find it interesting. My favorite composers are Hungarian, Polish, German, Russian, and Austrian. My favorite cuisines are Chinese, Indian, Mexican, French, and

American. My favorite clothiers are Italian. I love American movies, British musicals, and World history. I'm fascinated by the Holy Land, Stonehenge, Machu Picchu in Peru, the Pyramids in Mexico and in Egypt. And my best friend is Jewish.

I could go on and on and on but you get the point. My people are the people of this planet. I know it may sound too sugary for some of you, but that is the way I think and the only honest way that I see my life. And if I could go to another planet, maybe I would still feel happy to be an earthling, but probably then I would consider myself just another being in this wonderful universe.

Once you get rid of those obstacles and limits, you'll start seeing your fellow human beings as equals, and you'll break down some of the barriers that too many people try to hide behind. This is an important step on the road to happiness.

When you depart this world, you'll be remembered by your deeds, actions, and contributions to the well-being of mankind. The color of your skin, your religion, and national origin will not make a difference. So next time that you have to write down your race on paper, write human. You'll feel happier. Try it.

CHAPTER XIII

"Play It Again, Sam"

I would say that it's not a good idea to go through life bugging people. Especially the ones that help you feel happy, like your local pianist.

One thing I know about human nature is that if you tell someone — an acquaintance, an old friend, a relative, a coworker, anyone — that some particular habit of theirs bothers you, I can almost promise you that they'll do it more. Just to be cute, just to get a laugh. I'm telling you; they'll always do it even more often than before.

In the past, when I was playing at different hotels, once in a while I'd get a smart aleck who would come to the piano and either play a note without asking, in the middle of my work, or just do something silly in general. I used to make a point about it, but it would only get worse. Finally, I learned that the best way to deal with them is to ignore them. Eventually, these guys always get bored by the lack of attention and will leave, and then you're happy again.

But every once in a while, I've had to do something more drastic. One day a few years ago, I was playing the piano in Macy's Plaza in downtown Los Angeles and a man came to the piano and insisted that he wanted to play. He had that loony look in his eyes, so, reluctantly, I complied.

He started playing some nonsense music, if you can call it that, and "singing" made-up lyrics like "Shopping mall! I'm in a shopping mall!" After a few seconds, I asked him to leave and he just ignored me. So, I went to get security and I happened to see the head of security for the whole building.

He came to the piano, identified himself, and escorted the crazy guy out of the building. I thought that it was the end of the story. Well, the following day, a couple of guys came to my piano and told me that the "loony" guy from the day before was actually the well-known TV personality Tom Green, and he had been filming an "episode" or moment for his show with a hidden camera that was attached to his hat. I had a good laugh and I signed to allow them to air it in one of his programs. They did, and for a few days, more people told me about seeing me on TV (for approximately 30 seconds) than have commented on my career throughout all of my years combined. Go figure!

I guess one lesson Mr. Green helped get across is that the more you react to someone's annoying behavior, the more they'll do it. Let me explain using my own experiences. If I had one dollar for every time a person walked in front of my piano (in my many jobs over the years) while I'm playing As Time Goes By and said to me, "Play it again, Sam," I would be able to retire and buy The Peninsula, in cash. Whenever this happened, I used to complain to the nearest person to me, a coworker, another customer, a friend. Big mistake. That would only trigger more of the "Play it again, Sam" comments. The moment that I stopped caring, that would be the end of it. By the way, just for the record, that alleged line from the movie *Casablanca* never happened. Rick (Humphrey Bogart) never, ever says that in the movie. I have the movie. You can check it out.

Knowing human nature, this story is probably going to backfire on unsuspecting pianists all over the U.S. Some of you will now no doubt say to him or her, "Play it again, Sam." Just so you know, you will not get a smile from that innocent pianist!

A few nights ago, and this has happened a couple of times, I finished playing a Chopin Nocturne, a guy came over to my piano with his girlfriend and told me how much he loved that "Mozart" piece. I told him that it wasn't Mozart, that it was Chopin, well, he went into a very strange explanation on why it was Mozart. While I was listening to his nonsense reasons, all I could think was, the wheel is turning, but the hamster is dead.

The point of the story is that you are always going to find people who bug people. It sounds like a song, right? And the best solution is to ignore them. Sometimes it takes a little discipline to help you stay on course on the road to happiness.

CHAPTER XIV

Christmastime...and Other Times Too

One of the great contributors to my own happiness is my favorite time of the year: Christmastime.

If you don't celebrate Christmas, I'm sure that whatever joyful religious occasions you might celebrate are a great source of happiness for you, your friends and your family. And even if you're an atheist, I imagine that enjoying the holidays can still add a sense of well-being to your life. I'm just guessing here.

For me, the anticipation of a happy event in itself starts to trigger feelings of being happy. That sentiment can, if you choose to let it, linger for a while. Grab on to that feeling and enjoy the ride.

The best personal example of this I can give is Christmas. I start thinking about Christmas in the summer, when one of the cable channels has their "Christmas in July" sale. Additionally, there is a local store that puts their Christmas collection on display very early, in July and that begins the joyride for me. You see, Christmases throughout my life have provided me with some of my most beloved memories.

Of course, I realize that these feelings are not universally shared by everyone. As I've mentioned before, I always hear the yearly complainers in the malls, hotels and at work. They say, "It's getting earlier and earlier every year!" and "It's too stressful," and "I'm not ready to start thinking about Christmas." We've all heard the complaints. When I hear them, it's like they're saying to the world, "I'm not ready to feel good yet."

But Christmastime is just a personal example for me. In fact, there are many happy memories that I can call upon whenever I want. Like I've mentioned before, I collect happy memories, and oftentimes they come in handy.

Let me share a particular technique that I use. As a rule, when I start feeling stressed out about life, work, social circumstances, etc., I go to my memory bank and I withdraw whatever I need for the day and refresh my heart with those happy thoughts. It works like a charm. Try it, but be sure that you have deposited those thoughts in the past in your personal memory bank. If you think hard enough, I'm sure you'll find some, and it's never too late to keep making deposits, remember?

Really, try taking this small step. You know there are people who collect stamps, coins, cars, money, whatever is their pastime. I collect memories. Happy and wonderful memories.

It helps that somehow; I am lucky enough to not remember and focus on the bad moments in my life. As I've mentioned before, I tend to focus on the positive parts of life.

I am so thankful that I am this way. I know that not everyone is so lucky, and even that not everyone wishes to be like this. More than once I have heard people say, "It's good to be sad," and "It's good for you to feel down sometimes." Well, not for me. So far in my life I'm enjoying the ride, feeling very happy. And I sleep like a baby. Actually, I hope babies sleep this well!

So, why then would I change my outlook on life? I have a very basic philosophy about certain situations. Some people love to open up the back of a radio, TV, or other technical or mechanical instrument to look or mess around inside. Not me. If it isn't broken, I leave it alone. Same with life.

A few years ago, one lady told me, after only a couple of dates, "You are fooling yourself into believing that you can be that happy. It's not going to last." Guess what: it's still lasting and I'm still happy. Does it sound too simplistic? Too easy? Maybe, but the final analysis is that *it works*!

What I'm trying to say is that part of the reason I think I find it easy to stay positive is that my memory bank is filled to the brim with happy memories that I can retrieve whenever I feel like I need them. Of course, some of my favorites involve Christmas. In fact, I've already told you one of my all-time favorites: When my son was a little boy, the first sighting of Santa in the mall was a great source of joy for him. The memory of his smile and laughter has stayed alive and well in my memory bank. When necessary, I go make a withdrawal.

How about you? Do you have plenty of good things to remember? I think that if we look hard enough, we can all find something. In any case, start collecting memories in your personal memory bank. You can start today. Whatever gives you joy, whether it's Christmastime, music, a certain song, a phone call to a special friend, a letter, a painting, a sunset, your favorite pet, or simply looking up at the stars at night, find what gives joy to your heart and caresses your soul and then treasure that thought. Put it away in your memory and it'll be there for you when you need it the most. A collection of little (and big) happy moments, when they're all put together as your life flies by, can help you along on the path to happiness. It's all about recognizing the good and happy times.

Sometimes, during my performances at hotels during the summer, I play a soft Christmas carol. Most of the time, I get back some smiles and looks of peaceful feelings. I guess I'm not alone in treasuring Christmas, not matter what time of the year it is.

When those difficult days come my way as they always do, that night on my bed, after my nightly prayers, I go back to those cold evenings in winter during my childhood days and I vividly see my parents decorating our home for Christmas. I see myself playing Christmas carols on the piano and singing along with my three brothers. To me, that's a million-dollar memory, and it's available to me at will. Which memories will you think about?

CHAPTER XV

Caressing

Everybody, or most everybody, enjoys a hug,
a kiss, a soft touch, and a warm embrace…

…Unless it's unwelcome, I guess. But I'm talking about lovers, friends, family, siblings, and parents. Of course, one caress that is a bit harder to achieve is to touch someone's heart. Yes, it is harder to do, but I think it is worth the effort. That elusive feat of touching someone's heart can help them feel happy and loved.

Even though a physical caress is probably the first basic sensation we experience, and even though it is still something we enjoy, to attempt the caress of the heart is quite difficult. But once it happens, I believe that you have helped that person feel joy and happiness. So, how can you achieve this?

Let me begin by saying again that I consider myself extremely lucky and happy. I have always made a living by doing what I love to do the most: playing the piano. Besides the obvious fringe benefits — doing the job that I love, caressing my own soul with music, feeling that "going to work" is a great idea, wearing a nice suit every night, and working in a beautiful environment — there is also another benefit to my career that I consider more meaningful and important. Once in a while, I get to touch and caress somebody's heart and soul.

How can I be sure? Because people have been telling me so for many years — friends, strangers, family members, acquaintances, etc. I know that my day was not wasted when somebody comes to my piano and says to me, "Your music really touched me." Those are my favorite words. It reassures me that I am not wasting my life.

Find those moments in your personal life and you'll make somebody happy, including yourself. Of course, not everybody plays the piano. I know this. My father didn't play the piano, but he managed to make us feel happy. You can do it simply by listening to a friend, taking someone to a museum, pointing out a beautiful flower, bringing someone a book to read, or taking someone out to a concert or to dinner. The possibilities are endless, and the results are always the same: you can make someone feel better. Kind words, a reassuring talk, a mending of the wings of hope for a child or friend, those tools are available to everyone. Use them and you'll help someone feel happy. And, as an added benefit, you'll feel happy too. It's a win-win situation.

The seeds of happiness have a way to flourish in life at the most amazing moments. But you need to take the time to plant those seeds.

CHAPTER XVI

Time Flies When You're Having Fun

or

Time's Fun When You're Having Flies

I have never been bored in my life. This is surely another factor that contributes to my philosophy about happiness.

Time flies when you're having fun. One of my first days in the USA, I heard that expression. With my limited English, I wasn't sure of what "time flying" meant, but I got the gist of it. Now I recognize that when you use your creativity and productivity every day, or most days in your life, a couple of things happen: you never waste your time and you become incapable of being bored.

Boredom cannot live in a productive and creative mind, because creativity gives wind to the wings of your soul. I am happy to tell you that I truly don't know what it's like to feel bored. Intellectually I know what it means, but emotionally I don't.

During my years playing the piano in the daytime at Nordstrom and Macy's Plaza, I encountered many, many persons who, after a few visits to my piano, would confess that they were "bored." Bored with their jobs, their mates (sometimes), their routines, or their lives. The last statement was truly sad to hear.

Every day, during those jobs, I would see the same people, sitting in the same places, doing their same routines. I would see a lady reading a book every day and ripping off the pages that she would finish. I would see a man in a business suit walking from the entrance of the mall to the entrance of Macy's, forth and back, forth and back. I would see people of all ages and ethnic backgrounds, men and women, just hanging around.

My schedule was to play from 11:00 a.m. to 2:00 p.m., and I would see the same people every day. Some of them were retired and they enjoyed going to the mall to listen to my music. I always welcomed them. But some people were there just to take a two-hour "lunch break" (how did they get away with it?) and they would ask me the same exact questions every day.

For instance, there was a young man in his 20s working in the building who would ask me almost every day, "Do you teach?" And I would always say, "Not now. I'm too busy. Maybe in 10 years." After listening to this same question every single day for a while, one day I wrote on a piece of paper: "Not now. I'm too busy. Maybe in 10 years." He approached my piano and in the middle of his all-too-familiar question, I grabbed the paper out of my pocket and showed it to him. He never came back.

That situation reminds me of an Oscar Wilde's quote: "A true gentleman is one who is never unintentionally rude." I guess a bore is somebody who is never *intentionally* rude!

I also remember a young, handsome guy from Europe who was trying to become an actor. At first, I admired his tenacity in trying, because he came to the United States a few times in a short period. When he would lose his temporary jobs, he would come to my piano and ask me the most insane yet boring questions, like, "How would you make a living if you broke your arms?" and "Do you get paid for this?" He seemed to love my piano, but then he would confess that he was "bored out of his mind."

I think that the only way you can become bored is when your mind is not creating anything at all. No goals, no objectives, no intentions of improving the quality of your life, and no desire to make a difference in this world by trying to figure out ways to help your fellow human beings. I think that once you find meaning in your life and reasons for being, the concept of being bored gets thrown out the window.

So, time really flies when you are having fun, or as I prefer to say, when you are being productive. My days are so short, they seem to fly by along with the weeks and months, and sometimes I wish they were longer. That way I could do more writing, read more books, write more music, play more beautiful music, find ways to improve my life, and learn a bit more.

I especially wish that I had more time to read. In a funny or paradoxical way, the more I read books, the more I'm aware of my own ignorance. It's ironic but so true. That's why you should never be bored: there is *always* something that you could be learning!

As of the writing of this book, I haven't experienced the true feelings of being bored. That's one part of the human experience that I can do without. Maybe one way to find happiness is not to allow yourself to be bored. Keep busy, keep learning, keep your mind active and engaged. It's a simple concept that can set off a wonderful chain reaction that can be very pleasant and rewarding. You'll be happier.

CHAPTER XVII

Tennis, Chess, and Old Age

I am happy when I play tennis. For about one hour, I forget about bills, work, traffic, etc. All I think about is the fun of the game.

I'm not claiming that playing a game of tennis is a sure recipe for happiness for everybody, but for more than 30 years, my weekly (then daily), tennis match with my friend Bob has added immeasurable happiness to my days. Tennis is just a real example of something that I personally love.

I've met a lot of people who play sports on the weekends, whether it's basketball, scuba diving, tennis, or golf. (By the way, I read someplace a long time ago that golf is "a good walk spoiled." My brothers wouldn't like that description!) Anyway, a common thread among active people is that they seem, in my eyes, happier than those who would prefer to sit on the couch and watch TV.

Quite often, some of the people who came up to my piano in the malls would tell me about their weekends. I can tell you that they came in two types. One type included the ones who would say to me something like, "Friday night I went out and shot some pool with my friends, Saturday morning I went surfing and went out for dinner at night, and Sunday I played softball."

Then there was the other type. These people would say to me something like, "I just had a quiet weekend watching some TV and hanging around the house." Translation: "I did *nothing*, sat in front of the TV eating Doritos, and just waited for Monday to arrive." As a general rule, I would say that the people in the first group almost always appeared happier and more energetic than those in group two. Make your own conclusions.

Earlier in the book, I discussed calisthenics for the mind, and I mentioned chess. It's another "sport" that I love. Chess gives me the mental challenge that I love. I have read, and maybe you have too, that playing chess is one of the great ways to keep your mind sharp and focused. This remarkable game involves no luck — only thinking is required. You don't have to be physically strong. There's no height advantage. Muscles will not help you. In chess, you are equipped only with your mind.

Speaking of muscles, I have a T-shirt that I used to enjoy wearing once in a while. On the front, it says "Body by Mrs. Fields." Mrs. Fields is the founder of Mrs. Fields Bakeries, and I was addicted to her chocolate chip cookies. People always laugh when they see me wearing it. Don't get me wrong, I think that daily exercise is a way to stay healthy, and by staying healthy you increase your chances to be happy. Nothing is more important than health. But really, everything in moderation. Who doesn't love a good cookie now and then? Unfortunately, that T-shirt doesn't fit me anymore!

In the past, I have dated very, very physically fit ladies. They always exercised more than me, were generally younger than me, and fitter. Some of them worked out two to three hours after work every day to achieve that "perfect" body. The downside, in my opinion, is that they were always more tired than me. They would often say, "Antonio, we better not go out tonight, I worked out a lot and I'm really tired." But I wasn't tired. So, to a point, I guess getting in terrific shape might not be all that it seems. Who wants to spend all of their energy working out? Wouldn't you want some energy left over for other fun things? So, even it comes to exercise, I say everything in moderation.

OK, let's get back to the chess factor. Like I said, exercise is important, but I think the greatest form of exercise is for your mind.

I used to play chess everyday online with my son, now he is an attorney and very busy. The challenge of playing a game during the day is a good way to break up your routine. It helps exercise a different part of your brain. I really think it helps me keep my mind sharp. Plus, I have a good time. More ingredients for happiness.

Playing classical music on the piano is also good exercise. Maybe the ideal exercise, if you ask me. I move my fingers, my hands, my arms, my upper body, and even my lower body by using the foot pedals. I use my brain, by reading the music in front of me or by just remembering the notes of pieces that I know by heart. I use my soul to bring meaning and emotion to the music. I caress my heart by doing it. What sport can give you all that?

Maybe the idea of learning an instrument is a good idea for you too. It can add to your happiness and has the advantage of being an activity that you can do all by yourself. You don't need a partner to play the piano or the violin or the guitar. However, when you do find a good musical partner, it's pure joy. Happiness to the max.

Many years ago, when I lived in Tucson, Arizona, I was playing in a wonderful five-star restaurant called the Tack Room. One night, this lovely lady congratulated me on my piano playing. When I asked her, "Do you play the piano?" She said, "A bit." I had a funny (good) feeling about it and asked if she would like to play a piece for me. She went to the piano and started playing a piece by Liszt. I couldn't believe my ears. *A bit*?! She was a wonderful pianist. Her name was Elizabeth (now Elizabeth Pridonnoff). We began a good friendship and decided to play piano duets together each night after I finished playing at the restaurant. I would come over to her house and we would play Mozart, Beethoven, Brahms, Dvorak, etc., for hours and hours.

Many times, I would leave her house in the early morning and the look of some neighbor picking up his or her newspaper would be one of "I wonder what *you* did last night." Of course, little did they know that all we did was play the piano together! We never had an intimate relationship. At least not physically intimate, although I feel that we certainly connected musically and spiritually on a very deep level. Playing with her was always such a tremendous joy. It brought me such a sense of happiness that I wish I could put it into your heart so that you could know what I mean. Nowadays, I'm lucky that I found a fellow pianist and we play music for 4 hands one piano and for two pianos twice a week. I'm grateful for the joy of doing music together with my friend Sheryl.

That reminds me. Many years ago, while I was still living in Mexico City, I put together a piano recital. One of the pieces was the *Concerto for 4 Keyboards* (yes *four*) by Bach-Vivaldi. Imagine four concert grand pianos on one stage, all playing the glorious music of Bach. That is some kind of happiness that cannot really be described. The joy of playing that music with three other very talented pianists goes beyond description.

During my days in Tucson, I knew some older ladies who loved to play the piano, playing solos and duets with friends. Those old (chronologically speaking) ladies were some of the happiest, most positive, and cheerful people that I knew. I am sure that playing music was part of the reason for their happiness.

My first piano teacher, my maternal grandmother, used to play the piano quite often. And she loved it. By the look on her face during those moments of performing, I had the feeling that the arthritis and diabetes that were part of her daily life were forgotten. I think that she was a happy woman because she played the piano and loved her family.

Do you understand what I'm trying to say? Keep your mind active and you'll be happier. Remember, you are never too old to learn how to play a musical instrument or chess. These simple pleasures can be enjoyed by anybody.

I heard once that age matters only for cheese and wine. How true! For example, I had the pleasure, the privilege, and the honor to see and hear one of the greatest guitarists of the 20th Century, Andres Segovia, in concert here in Los Angeles. He was in his 90s, but onstage the person playing that beautiful guitar was not an old man. He was simply a beautiful human being. Granted, he started playing very young, but that is not always the case. By the way, I managed to go backstage, shake his hand and talk alone with him for a few minutes. I think you'll enjoy the story. After the concert, I went to the door backstage outside the hall and there were many people already there trying to get in to see the Maestro. Of course, the man at the entrance told all of us that he wasn't receiving visitors. Well, I wrote something on the back of one of my business cards and I gave it to the guard and I just told him to please give the card to Mr. Segovia. Believe or not, to the bewildered looks of everybody around me, after a few minutes, he came back and said "Mr. Castillo de la Gala, please follow me". I did and I saw the great Segovia seating alone in his dressing room. We exchanged a few words, he knew Manuel M. Ponce, the teacher of my piano teacher and he played some of his works for guitar as part of his concert repertoire. After a few minutes, I didn't want to overstay my welcome and I left. Very happy and honored to meet one of the great musicians of the 20th Century. What did I write on the back of my business card that open the door for me? I wrote that I just came from Mexico City to listen to his recital. That's it. Of course, I didn't mention that I had come from Mexico City a few years before.

I have a great deal of admiration for Anna Mary Robertson, better known as Grandma Moses. That remarkable woman had to support her five surviving children by doing many jobs, until she discovered embroidering. That new job made her happy. And when her arthritis made it too difficult to hold the embroidery needles, Grandma Moses reinvented herself. She started painting. She started painting in her 70s, and at age 80 she had her first solo show. She was 101 years old when she passed away.

Don't you see? You can start playing piano or other instrument that you always wanted to try at any age. If you think painting might be a source of happiness for you, try that. The point is to keep busy, to stay creative. Keep using your mind.

Let me give you another example. Dorothy "Dodo" Cheney was born in 1916. She was an avid tennis player. She died in 2014, at 98. Probably had more trophies than Novak Djokovic, Rafael Nadal and Roger Federer put together. She had over 390 national titles!

When I hear people talking about how when they turn 65, they plan on retiring and doing nothing, I just want to go to them and tell them about life and what can happen in the so-called old age. My grandmother used to say, "*Viejos los cerros y reverdecen.*" It means, "Old are the hills and they will be green again." Isn't that beautiful?

Would you like some more examples? There are plenty:

When Colonel Harland Sanders turned 65, he started Kentucky Fried Chicken.

At 65, Sir Winston Churchill became Prime Minister of the United Kingdom.

At 70, Golda Meir was elected Prime Minister of Israel.

Also, at 70, E. B. White wrote his classic children's story, *The Trumpet of the Swan.*

At 75, Mary Harris "Mother" Jones, the labor leader, helped found the Industrial Workers of the World.

Also, at age 75, Claudio Arrau, one of the great concert pianists of all time, gave 110 concerts!

At 78, Bertrand Russell, the great British philosopher, essayist, and social critic, was awarded the Nobel Prize for literature. By the way, at age 85, he introduced the international peace symbol.

At 80, Jessica Tandy and George Burns won their first Oscars.

Also, at 80, Leopold Stokowski, the great orchestra conductor, founded the American Symphony Orchestra.

At age 85, Celestine III was elected Pope.

At 90, Sophocles wrote one of the greatest dramas in history, *Oedipus at Colonus*.

Also, at 90, Jacob Coxey Sr., a fighter for the rights of unemployed workers, finally got to deliver his speech — planned 50 years earlier — in the Capitol.

At 95, the wonderful dancer and choreographer Martha Graham premiered her last work in choreography, *Maple Leaf Rag*.

Also, at 95, Mother Jones (yes, her again) wrote her autobiography.

At the age of 100, the great stage actress from the British theater, Gwen Ffrangcon-Davies, appeared in the movie *The Master Blackmailer*. She was also made a Dame by the Order of the British Empire.

Also, at the age 100, Mr. Ichijirou Araya did something that I know I will never even try: he climbed Mount Fuji.

For sure, retirement is not in my vocabulary. I wonder if that way of thinking keeps my thoughts and dreams fresh and full of hope. I hope it made you happy to hear about these amazing endeavors. Who knows, maybe you'll even be happy doing some of them!

Whatever you do, if it makes you tired and doesn't allow you to enjoy life, in my opinion, it doesn't work. My regular diet of exercise is limited to stretching, my treadmill, lifting some weights and my tennis. That's it, no more. My motto is: "No pain…good." One tiny piece of advice that I know it will keep you healthier, wash your hands, very often during the day, which I do. The first time, when I wake up, and the last time, just before I go to bed at night.

So, start those calisthenics of your mind today. You'll probably stay sharper and perhaps live longer.

CHAPTER XVIII

"Where there is music, there can be no evil."

—Cervantes, Don Quixote

In my opinion, one of the greatest sources of joy and happiness for all of us is music.

Music is a universal language for which translations are not necessary. Perhaps music is the collective voice of all humanity. I think it represents and reveals the best in all of us.

When I sit at the piano and play Chopin, there is nothing wrong with the world. Nothing hurts. The world is fine, and problems just fall away. Even if for only a few minutes, music can give you the kind of joy and peaceful feelings that are so welcome in our lives. I believe a house with music is a happier house than one without. Of course, there are, like everything else in life, exceptions to this "rule." E. M. Cioran wrote, "Music is the refuge of souls ulcerated by happiness." I guess he probably wasn't a happy camper.

I always imagine that if I would travel to another world in another galaxy, and a being from another planet asked me, "What is the best that you humans can offer to the universe?" then I would probably play him Beethoven's Ninth Symphony.

People around my piano are always telling me, "If I got to live my life all over again, I would probably learn how to play an instrument." I always tell them, "Why don't you start tomorrow, or better yet, why not today?" You can spend your whole life making plans or you can start living by making your dreams a reality. Again, I believe happiness is a state of being that you have to pursue, try, and learn.

So, if you're thinking about learning an instrument, give it a try. Music is a beautiful, magical thing. I think there is an invisible connection in our collective humanity that transcends time and space when we listen to great music. Think about it: Listening to Mozart can give you the same or close to the same kind of emotions that people who lived in his time were feeling.

When I close my eyes, and immerse myself in the immortal sounds of Tchaikovsky or Rachmaninoff and their beautiful, almost painful melodies, I feel the common thread of all humanity. Maybe music creates a sense of being part of the whole human race. I know it may sound sappy to many of you, but I have always felt a connection with the joys and suffering of all of us through music. I also think that the more we share music with our friends from all over the world, the less separated we feel from them.

Again, I can't help but remember my grandmother playing Chopin. I am sure that her arthritis temporarily went away from her body, or at least from her thoughts, even if only for a few minutes. All my life, I have heard about the healing power of music. Much has been written on the subject and this is not the place to go into detail about it, but I will share with you a very powerful experience in my life about that subject.

While I was playing at Macy's Plaza, I encountered thousands of people over the years around my piano. One individual comes to mind now. Sometimes, I would see this frail, gentle-looking man sitting close to the piano. After a couple of hours of listening, he would nod, give me a warm smile, and then slowly walk away. For a few weeks, things went on that way.

Finally, on a quiet morning when I didn't have the usual crowd around the piano, the man approached me and shook my hand. As I felt his very thin hands, he looked at me and with tears in his eyes, he said: "I just want to thank you for the Chopin that you just played. You see, I have terminal cancer and my doctor said that I don't have much time left. A couple of days from that doctor's visit, I walked into this mall, which is rare for me because I don't like malls and I don't have the energy or the time to waste, but I did and I started to listen to your music. I was completely drawn to it and sat close by. Pretty soon I found out that you come here five days a week and so I started to do the same. I have to tell you that, believe it or not, when you play classical music, I don't think about my physical pain. I just feel calmer and better. You truly have given more time to me and I thank you for that."

After that emotional day, he always stopped by to say hello and to thank me. He didn't like to talk much about his life and he was probably too physically tired to do so, but I remember that he was from Poland, so maybe the music of Chopin, who was born in Poland, had a special healing quality for him or reminded him of his childhood. Unfortunately, I have no idea of the details of his life, but his kind words are still vivid to me.

I do know that this man was, like me, a firm believer in the power of "good music," as he called it, to heal. It turns out that researchers may be proving us right. I just read an article about a study that was published in the journal *Medical Science Monitor*. In part, the researchers concluded: "[M]aking music has the potential to reverse the human stress response at the genomic level" (*International Musician Newspaper*, April 2005). Sounds about right to me!

I grew up playing piano and music was always present throughout my childhood. If you would ever meet me and my three brothers, you'd find that we are all very happy human beings. Coincidence? I don't think so.

Before you go to the next chapter, try something. Play a little Chopin on your CD player (or better yet, play my classical CD!). Let the beauty of music help you find and enjoy happiness. Find the right music for you and it will ennoble your heart.

CHAPTER XIX

T.G.I.F.? More Like T.G.I.T.

Not too long ago, T.G.I.F. stood for "Thank God It's Friday." Today, so as not to risk "offending" anyone of the PC crowd, they've changed it to "Thank Goodness It's Friday." Well, I say "T.G.I.T.: Thank God It's Today!"

I think another element that can affect your pursuit of happiness has a lot to do with the various influences that always pop into your life. Whether you like it or not, I think that a large part of our lives, our surroundings, and our obligations, not to mention TV, radio, the Internet, friends, and just people in general, are not always conducive to our goal of being happy. But you can do your best to not let them bring you down.

Let me explain. So many people focus on what day it is, or on whether or not it's a weekend or weekday, or on what the weather is like outside, and they let these outside factors affect how they feel on the *inside.* But when you love your life and your job, as I do, it really doesn't matter what day of the week it is, or what month, or what season. Life is just more pleasurable, interesting, and yes, fun. As you know by now, my work is one of the great pleasures of my life.

Still, everywhere I look, everyone seems to be obsessed with these trivial factors that they cannot change anyway, particularly the weather. When I'm on my treadmill, once in a while I'll tune in to a local TV channel. From the very beginning of the news program to its very end, I'll hear reports about the weather and how they say it's going to affect my weekend. For me, because I am from Mexico, where they don't really care about the weather, and because I now live in beautiful Southern California, it doesn't really concern me that much. I know, no matter what the weatherman or woman tells me, that 99.9% of the time, it's going to be great outside. Just great.

If you were born in the USA, especially outside of California, you're probably much more interested in the weather than I am, and rightly so, the weather probably affects you more than it does me.

It reminds me of a couple stories. Many years ago, I was playing the piano in a band with my brothers in Acapulco, Mexico, at a beautiful hotel, The Plaza Internacional Hyatt Regency Acapulco, a wonderful, gorgeous place with amazingly good weather throughout the whole year. It was fun to watch local TV because they didn't have a weatherman. Instead, at some point in the broadcast, the person reading the news would simply say something like, "Tomorrow we're going to have another beautiful day in Acapulco." That would be the entire "weather report."

Like I said, for Americans, the weather report gets a little more… involved. One day, while going to eat breakfast in the dining room of the hotel that I was performing and staying at, I noticed that at the front desk, they had a display with the temperatures of all the major American cities: New York, Los Angeles, Chicago, Washington, D.C., Dallas, etc. Even though the hotel had an international clientele — at one point, they had guests from 35 different countries! — the display only showed temperatures of American cities. I asked the front desk girl why this was the case, and she said to me, "The only people who ask about the weather are Americans." Surprised, I asked her what she meant, and she said, "I was curious too, so I asked one of our American guests who was inquiring about the weather in Dallas, 'Are you from Dallas?' and she said, 'No, I just like to know how the weather is there now. I have a friend who lives there.'"

We continued talking about it with another lady who worked at the front desk and came to the conclusion that Americans must not be able to go directly to breakfast before checking the weather in the U.S. and commenting on the different temperatures in those cities. I thought the whole thing was funny, but now that I live here in America, I do realize how important the weather is for Americans. Well, sort of (remember, I do live in L.A.!).

But even here, people get peculiar with the weather. To me it is very funny to see how people react when one tiny drop of rain falls in Los Angeles, which is rare. Martians could be landing on the White House lawn, or a man could have just walked on Mars for the first time. The person reading the news will tell you at the top of the broadcast that they have a "Storm Watch" update. You're probably used to it, but to me, it's very, very funny.

I also noticed something that I'm sure affects people's psyches. The TV and radio broadcasts will tell you, as soon as Monday arrives, about the prospect of the weather "for the weekend." See, everybody is waiting for the weekend like it's some kind of panacea that will cure all of your problems and take you away from your daily routine.

I know it's true that Monday morning is not a happy time in most places in the world. You know all the jokes about the Monday blues, or the comments like "I can't believe it's already Monday again" that you hear from friends, coworkers, and the media in general. Even in Mexico, there is an old expression that, loosely translated, says, "Hens don't lay eggs on Mondays."

But when you find a job that is also your passion, your life changes dramatically and you become happier. It doesn't matter then if it's Monday or Friday. It doesn't matter if it's raining a little outside. I promise you that once you start focusing on your goals in life and you put your mind and heart in it, the day of the week and even the month will hardly make a difference to your well-being.

In fact, I have my own personal way to look at all the months of the year. Try to focus on the positives of each month. Each one makes me happy in its own way.

In January, I'm excited because, to begin with, I made it another year. And of course, it's a time to renew goals. The excitement and the prospects of the year ahead are the fuel that drives the engine of my dreams. I love January.

February has a different color to me. It's the month of romance, with Valentine's Day arriving in the middle of the month. It's a nice chance for guys and ladies to be extra nice to each other and to get those obligatory flowers. Personally, I like to give flowers for no special occasion, not just because it's Valentine's Day. People who know me give me chocolates, one of the great pleasures in my life. By February, the winter is almost over and the crisper weather in L.A. is ideal for my tennis game. Also, my second grandson, Alexander, was born in February. I love February.

March has a special meaning for me also. It's the month of my birthday. I was born on March 2nd, and according to my mother, it was Carnival time in Veracruz, Mexico. Maybe that was a good omen for my never-ending optimism and *joie de vivre*. March is also the beginning of spring, and spring is all about the return of flowers and, for my own personal pleasure, the Dodgers. I can still hear the voice of Vin Scully and the promise of a new baseball season just around the corner. I am always happy to be in Dodger Stadium watching a game, eating my Dodger dogs and maybe some nachos. It's a wonderful little escape to a fun time when we can all be kids again. I love March. I miss the wonderful voice of Vin.

April is the month when spring is wearing its best dress. It's the time of Easter, with all the people in church with their nice outfits, and with Easter egg hunts going on all over the place. When my son was a little boy, it was the time to buy eggs and paint them the old-fashioned way, one by one. It's a happy time for children and a renewal of our own childhood reflected in the joy of their faces. I love April.

Where I am from, May is a very important month. In Mexico, they call May "*el mes de las flores*," or "the month of the flowers." May 1st is Labor Day in Mexico. May is also the month to remember mothers on Mother's Day, May 10th. And May 15th is the "Day of the Teacher." (In Mexico, holidays are always on the same date every year, except for Easter, of course). And you may be familiar with Cinco de Mayo, May 5th, a Mexican holiday that many Americans have a good time celebrating, for some reason. That's OK with me. It just means another excuse to laugh, share good times with friends, and maybe sing a song or two. I love May.

June is the halfway mark of the year, a time when I do some reevaluating of my life's goals and aspirations. June is summertime, meaning vacation time for children and many adults. The amusement parks are full of people and I personally don't mind seeing all the happy faces around. Also, somehow, I always write music in June. I love June.

July is the month to celebrate America's independence. I do not take the Fourth of July for granted. To me, it is a reminder of our freedoms and of how fortunate we are to live in a country that is, in my humble opinion, a unique experiment, a true melting pot where anything is possible, a fertile ground to allow all of your dreams to grow, as long as you're willing to work hard and live an honest life. It's a time to consider what makes this country so great. I love July.

August is a month with no celebrations that I am aware of. But the fact that I made it through to August at all is reason enough to celebrate for me. In August, I put myself into high gear concerning my goals. I try to accomplish as much as I can. August has a special energetic appeal to me. I love (not much) August.

September is the month that my son Antonio (Antonio Castillo, III) was born. That makes it a very special month. Back in Mexico, it is also the month to celebrate Mexican Independence Day. It's also back-to-school time. You'll probably hate me for saying this, but I *loved* going to school. The prospect of learning, especially when I was a student at the National Conservatory of Music in Mexico City, was just wonderful for me. I was always very grateful for the opportunity to learn music and polish my skills as a pianist. I love September.

October is a month full of promise, for me. When I start seeing the first Halloween decorations, to me it is warm-up time for Christmas. It may sound early to you, but in October I am already in the Christmas spirit. It's a wonderful time of year for me. My son used to get so excited with Halloween and planning what costume to wear at school that the memories of those days still bring a smile to my face. Remember, just as some people collect stamps or coins, I collect happy memories. Good ones like these. I love October.

November means it's just about Christmastime. I know it's early, but that's when I start playing Christmas songs, shop for the Castillo Family Christmas Card, finish the gift shopping for the season, and count down the days until Thanksgiving. We didn't have that holiday in Mexico, but Thanksgiving is a unique holiday in America that truly has no barriers, no matter what your ancestry or background is. It is the day to give thanks — *gratitude* — so it has special appeal to me. It's a wonderful holiday for all of us to enjoy. Plus, there's the food! I love November.

December is my favorite month. My first grandson, Antonio Castillo, IV was born on this month. I know I've mentioned Christmas three months in a row now, but I love it that much, and December is truly Christmastime, no doubt about it. December is a month that usually brings me huge amounts of joy and happiness. I think of all the sweet and sometimes sad memories of my loved ones who are gone. I was very lucky as a child. Even though we didn't have much money, my parents and grandparents always made sure that we had a great Christmas. Our Christmases were and are like the ones you probably see in the movies. Lots of music and singing around the piano, plenty of homemade cookies, lots of food and presents, and, for me, the added joy that I get when I play those timeless carols that bring smiles to (most) people and a look of nostalgia and memories of time gone by for so many friends. I love December.

Don't let outside forces dictate your inner feelings so easily. What does it really matter what day it is? Every day you are alive is the right time to pursue your dreams. Instead of obsessing about the "weekend weather," try thinking about your goals in life. Cross the river of life by placing stones where you can step across the way. From January to February, give yourself little milestones to step on. Do the same from February to March, etc., etc. By giving yourself attainable goals, you will connect the days, weeks, months, and years in a very smooth way. You'll be too happy to be worried about the weather each weekend. Every time that I hear, "T.G.I.F.," I remember to say to myself, "Thank God it's today! Thank God I'm alive."

Try it! I bet you'll already feel happier.

CHAPTER XX

The Genie in the Bottle
(*Carpe Diem!*)

What would you do if you found a bottle on the beach and a genie popped out to grant you three wishes? What wishes would you ask for?

Whenever someone asks me that question, my answer is always the same: I would say to the genie, "Get back in your bottle." Yes, I get some funny looks like I'm crazy or something, but I'm used to that. Well, of course I could ask for a few wishes: playing at Carnegie Hall, playing at Disney Hall with the L.A. Philharmonic, winning an Oscar....

You get the drift. Of course, there are things I want. But even though I am a dreamer, I figure it's up to me to attain whatever goals I have in my life. See, when you love your job, when you do something that truly makes you happy for a living, you have no time to complain. That's why I would tell the genie to get back in his bottle.

What about you? Remember, the genie question is a way to get you to think about the real questions you should be asking yourself, the big questions, like: "What am I going to do with my life?" "Where am I going?" "How am I going to make a living?" If you have an idealistic nature, you might add: "How can I make a difference in this world?"

The way I see it, I guess I am extremely lucky because I do what I love to do and I get paid for doing it. As an added bonus, every time that someone tells me that my music touched their heart or that they feel better after having listened to me play, those kind words are priceless and fill me with joy. To think that by playing my piano, I can touch someone's life and hopefully add a little joy or a sense of hope to their personal dreams, well, I wish I could convey how great that feels. It makes me feel like my life has meaning and purpose. I guess you could say that if life is a theater, I much prefer to be on the stage performing instead of sitting in the audience watching.

It's very important to me, and I hope you feel the same way about yourself, that my presence in this world will hopefully have a positive effect on the people who cross my path. That is one of my reasons for being. I want to fully love and be loved, to experience joy and happiness, to learn as much as I can about my fellow human beings, and to not waste my precious life staying idle.

Next time you think about how much you don't like your job, maybe you should play the genie game. Try it, you have nothing to lose. Imagine that you are walking alone on a secluded beach and you find the proverbial bottle. You open it up and poof, out comes the genie. The genie says only one thing: "I will grant you your dream job; what is it?" That's all. You get one wish, and that wish would be your ideal job. Now, before you answer the genie, think hard about what you would love to do for the rest of your life. What would make you happy? What would give your life meaning? No matter how silly or outrageous your dream is — what is it?

Maybe it is to play professional sports, or to be a writer, a painter, a singer, a farmer, a carpenter, a photographer, or a teacher. You only have one shot, so make sure you give an honest answer. If you don't have an answer right away, it's OK. It only means that you are still discovering yourself and trying to figure out your dreams.

If that is the case, tell the genie to wait. It could be hours, days, weeks, months, or years. In some cases, it could be a lifetime, but the adventure of trying to define your dreams and goals is probably the most exciting adventure that you'll ever take. Right there, by taking that first step, things will start to look better for you. Your mind and body are going to be focused on finding the answer to what is one of the most important personal questions of your life.

If, on the other hand, you have a quick answer, say it out loud and start working on it. I have had the pleasure to talk to different people who "found the genie" and followed their dreams, and they're very happy.

I used to talk to a gentleman in his 60s who would come around to my piano during my years playing at Macy's Plaza. He always told me during my breaks that music helped him dream his dreams. One day I asked him about those dreams. He was a businessman, very well dressed, so I assumed that he was doing well, financially speaking. He would tell me that he always wanted to paint nature, and how he was sad that he never did it. I would say to him, "You're not dead, so why don't you try it?" He would always then bring up his obligations to his job, family, etc.

Another day, I asked him about his family. He told me that the kids were out of the house, all married and living out of state. His wife was retired. I asked him what in the world was stopping him from following his dreams. And he said: "I'm probably too old to start all over again."

I told him that he wouldn't be starting all over again, but just opening another chapter in the book of his life. I wanted to know specifically what he dreamed of painting, and he mentioned something about painting the beautiful Arizona desert.

One time I said to him, "You have *nothing* to lose by quitting your job." After all, he had already told me about his retirement plan, so I was sure it wouldn't be a problem. I also asked him if he had talked with his wife about his dreams. And he said, "No, actually I have never mentioned those desires to paint to her. I did briefly when we were dating many years ago, but then we got busy with life."

So, I gave him some unsolicited advice. I said to him: "Please, tonight, tell her all these things that you told me about painting the Arizona desert. You might be pleasantly surprised." I never saw him at the mall again.

For a while, I was feeling a bit worried that I may have pressed a bit too hard about something as personal as following dreams, but quickly I forgot about him. But after a couple of years, during one of my evenings performing at the Hotel Bel-Air, a kind-looking man came to my piano and said to me, "There is nothing as beautiful as the Arizona desert, and I am putting it on my canvas."

It was my friend from Macy's Plaza.

It turns out that he did talk to his wife. He quit his job and they moved to Arizona, I think to Sedona. He started painting and I assume he is still doing it. He told me that he actually sold some of his paintings in open markets and that he was the happiest man on the face of the earth. He said his wife loved walking during the cool autumn evenings and that she had been exploring the surrounding places near their home on the outskirts of the city. He also said to me, "Thank you very much, from the bottom of my heart, for not letting me forget my life's dreams."

To tell the truth, I didn't really do anything. I only wanted to remind him of his early life goals because I have been lucky enough to achieve my own. He did all the work; he and his wife took all the necessary steps for pursuing their life dreams. He found his genie in the bottle.

I could give you countless examples of people that I have met who have followed their life goals. My friend Becky had long wanted to move to the Napa Valley and grow her own grapes and start her own wine business. She did it.

My friend Javier was a bartender in a restaurant. He always talked about how he wanted to photograph the running of the bulls in Pamplona. Well, he did it, and now he's a full-time photographer who travels all over the world.

My friend Armando, who was a valet parking attendant at a restaurant here in Los Angeles, always wanted to be a tour guide around the pyramids in his native Guatemala. The last I heard, he was enjoying himself and doing just that. And on and on and on.

There are no dreams too big for you to try to achieve. There are only the limitations that you probably put in front of yourself. Talk to the genie in the bottle today. Follow your dreams. Make yourself happy. Carpe diem!

I love that old phrase. *Carpe diem.* Centuries ago, Horace wrote in his *Odes*, "*Carpe diem, quam minimum credula postero,*" which means, "Seize the day, trusting as little as possible to the morrow." In Horace's poem, the speaker asks Leuconoe to make the most of the present and to stay away from astrologers. Over time, the celebrated phrase was shortened to carpe diem.

I think that Horace's advice is as relevant today as it was in his time. Make the most of today. Don't cheat yourself or anybody else of whatever the present (that lovely word that also means gift) might offer you. Yesterday is only a memory — hopefully a good one. Tomorrow is a hope. You have to grab today while it's here and just do whatever you are planning to do with your life.

Having regrets for whatever happened or didn't happen yesterday is a waste of time. Worrying about tomorrow, a very popular pastime, will do nothing to make you feel happy. But you have today.

I remember that when I was living in Tucson, there was a very nice couple who would come every weekend to see me play piano at the Tack Room. They always told me about their fast-growing boys and how much they weighed. At the time, I had no idea why they always told me their sons' height and weight, but I guess it's just one of those American customs that, in my early years in the USA, was new to me.

They also used to say to me, "We're going to have you come over for dinner at our home very soon. We are just doing some remodeling and as soon as we're done, we'll have you over." Well, after more than three years of listening to that story, I never went to their home for dinner. They were always "almost finished with the remodeling." Eventually I moved to Los Angeles and of course that was the end of that possible dinner.

To me it was kind of funny, because every time that I saw them, I knew they were going to tell me the new height and weight of their two sons, and I also knew that the would-be invitation to dinner would immediately follow.

You can spend a lifetime making plans to invite someone for dinner, or telling the friend you really want to see that one day soon you'll grab that cup of coffee, or convincing yourself that you'll read that book when you have the time, or postponing that trip you always planned on taking until next year, etc., etc.

The moment to do all those things is now. Today! We do not have the guarantee of being alive tomorrow. That's why, when that chocolate truffle is in front of me begging to be eaten, I don't wait for tomorrow. Now is the right time.

So, remember, *carpe diem*, seize the moment, the day, the opportunity. Grab the gift of the present and always use it wisely. Take active steps to make yourself happy now, while you can.

CHAPTER XXI

No Mexicans on TV!

*Do you really want TV, movies, and
"celebrities" to dictate your happiness?*

A few years ago, while driving home from the Beverly Hills Hotel, where I was the resident pianist for more than nine years (I'll tell you how that came about in a bit!), I was listening, as I still do, to talk radio. The program that day was focused on "the lack of minorities on TV." A caller was complaining about the fact that there were not enough Latinos on television. He wished that there were more so that "we could have some role models to imitate."

Well, needless to say, I was angered by those comments, so I called in to the program. I managed to get through and I was put on the air.

Because of my strong opposition to their comments, the other caller and the host were very surprised that I was a Mexican. I told them that I wouldn't care one bit if I never saw a Mexican or Salvadorian or African-American, Asian, European, Jew, Eskimo, Native American, Martian, etc., etc., fill in the blank, on TV.

That caused *them* to become outraged, and the caller asked me, "Aren't you proud of your race?" By now, dear reader, you can probably guess what my response was: "My race is human." After much snickering and nervous laughter, they told me, "Come on, be serious, I mean '*La Raza*.'" (Remember, this means "the race," in Spanish.) I told them again the same response, and then I elaborated on my personal philosophy, and how I don't let TV or other media dictate my own sense of worth or influence my well-being.

The way I see it, TV has no — nada, zilch, zero — effect on how I view myself or feel about myself. I don't need to see Mexicans on TV to feel happy about who I am. I really don't. I would welcome them and wish them the best, but it would never affect my own sense of happiness. I don't need a "role model" from the movies. I don't need to see a Latino in prime time so that I can feel "proud."

On other talk shows that I have managed to call in to, the other callers are usually very angry at me for not feeling "proud" of my race. But I always give the same answer. To me, there is no reason for people to be proud of the color of their skin, which we are all born with by accident. The same goes for the language that you happened to grow up with. There is no achievement on my part regarding where I was born, who my parents were, or what color my hair is.

I think that to feel "proud" about your "race" or ethnicity puts tremendous limitations on the way that you'll view the whole world as a unity of mankind. The prouder that you feel about certain things you probably had nothing to do with instead of real achievements, the more you won't be able to appreciate and understand all of the wonderful differences and unique attributes that exist among all human beings.

Fortunately, I don't have those ideas, therefore I think I have a more open attitude and worldview. There are many ways to find "role models" in your personal life. Look toward your parents, siblings, grandparents, teachers, extended relatives, friends, books.

I think that in books and in the stories of all the achievements of so many people who have made this a better world, in those pages you'll find plenty of inspiration and role models that will help shape your life to be happier and more fulfilling.

I was probably very lucky to have very supportive parents and grandparents who were the biggest supporters of my goal to become a pianist. Add to that my always tremendous passion for books and reading and you probably have a prescription for a sense of confidence, self-worth, and happiness.

I really don't try to emulate or copy "celebrities." They really don't affect my life. Sports figures are not role models for me. I may admire some athletes' discipline and I could surely learn a thing or two about tenacity from some of them, but trying to make them a role model is not something I am preoccupied with.

So, beginning today, stop whining about not seeing someone who "looks like you" on TV or elsewhere, as I heard that caller complain on a talk show. Create your own destiny. Find your own dreams. Search for your own goals.

Now go ahead and go after them. You don't need to see someone who looks like you on TV or in the movies in order to feel good about yourself. When you turn off the TV or leave the movie theater, you return to your own life, and the people on the little or big screen have long gone about their own. They don't know you and they probably never will.

If you look around carefully in real life, you'll see plenty of people who go to work everyday, raise their children, do a decent job, try to better themselves, and hopefully make this a better world for the rest of us. Those countless unknown persons, who are not celebrities or movie stars or sports stars, are the true role models.

This is another reason that I am a very happy person. I am not looking for people who look like me to make myself feel better. I am happy to be Antonio.

You can be happy to be yourself. You are a unique, one-of-a-kind being in the universe. There is no one like you in the whole world, so be your best role model to yourself. Be the best that you are capable of being.

After all, there is only one *you*. Doesn't that make you happy?

CHAPTER XXII

A Beggar with a Stick

Growing up in Mexico, I often heard the expression "Limosnero y con garrote," which means, "A beggar with a stick."

"A beggar with a stick" is a typical, and very funny, in my opinion, old Mexican expression that encompasses some humorous but true philosophical thoughts. It means that quite often on our travels through life, we'll try to do something good or kind towards another person, only to have it backfire and bite us in the butt, probably making us feel unhappy. You cannot let the "beggars with sticks" ruin your desire for kindness or mess up your feelings of happiness.

Remember the story I told you about how I played piano at someone's

house as a child, but the people there were rude and didn't even pay any attention? As I told you earlier, my grandmother, when we got back to our house, said to me, "Don't worry TOÑITO (a nickname from my parents), honey was never meant for a donkey's mouth." Well, she also went on to tell me stories of great pianists and composers who sometimes were ignored (or worse) during their performances by certain members of the audience. She said to me, "Sometimes what they (those pianists and composers) did was like throwing flowers to the pigs. It was a waste of nice flowers and the pigs didn't care about it."

I usually try to remember those stories when I am confronted with situations where I feel my efforts are not appreciated. I'll give you an example.

A few years ago, playing at the Polo Lounge at the Beverly Hills Hotel, one lady, in a party of five or six, asked me if I could make her birthday special by playing a song from *West Side Story*. I said to her, "I'll do better than that; I'll play for you a medley of a few songs from that wonderful show."

Allow me to backtrack a little bit. A few years before, in Mexico City, I happened to have a very interesting experience regarding that show. An American theater company came to Mexico to do *West Side Story* for a 30-day stay in that country. Their pianist got sick the first day that they arrived in Mexico. One of the producers of the show called the National Conservatory of Music and asked if a student pianist would be willing to have a month-long gig as the pianist for the show and make some money.

My teacher, the director of the Conservatory, Mr. Joaquin Amparan — a very distinguished, elegant, and marvelous teacher — asked me if I wanted the job. It was a heck of a challenge because the pianist was required to play the "whole score," as they said on the phone, with only a couple days of rehearsal.

Those who are familiar with sheet music and have seen the marvelous Leonard Bernstein composition will know right away that it is not "Twinkle, Twinkle Little Star." It is a hard and complicated score, quite intricate and beautiful. In my opinion, it is probably the best American Broadway show ever written.

To make a long story not too long, I decided to go for it and I did it.

It became a wonderful experience and I still have a copy of the score autographed by the cast, including the conductor, who was a student of

Bernstein; Chita Rivera; and other members of the cast who were either in the Broadway production or in the movie version of the show.

Because of that situation, I still know the score pretty well. It has many memorable songs that are still part of the requests of audiences all over.

So, back to my story at the Polo Lounge.

Needless to say, I played a rather long medley that probably included most of the famous songs from the show. All in all, it was about 15 minutes of uninterrupted music from *West Side Story*, and at the end, the audience at the Polo Lounge gave me a very nice ovation.

Very happy with myself, I approached the table to say happy birthday to the lady who made the request and, I hoped, to see a happy smile. You can imagine my surprise when I approached the table and she looked at me with a forced smile and said, "It was nice, but you didn't play my favorite song in the show!"

A beggar with a stick, I thought to myself. She was disappointed and I figured she was the kind of person who would be almost impossible to please, because she would always manage to see the other side of the coin, the unhappy side, and she would probably find it quite easily. To me, the lesson was simple. I remembered my grandmother's words. You just can't make everybody happy all the time, no matter how hard you try.

So sometimes you will come across people like that. One day, I saw a man asking for money because he was hungry and "hadn't eaten for a few days," as he told me. It happened in my early days in Tucson, probably around the second year of my life in the USA. He was at the entrance of a supermarket, and while I was shopping, I decided to do my good deed for the day and I bought him some apples, bananas, and some canned meat. Very happy with myself, I gave it to him on the way out.

He took them, but he said to me, "I need cash, man, cash for food!" with an angry tone of voice, and then he walked away. Well, I learned a tough lesson that day just by doing the right thing.

Talking about that story with my brothers some time ago, we all remembered a funny incident that happened when we were children living with our parents in Veracruz, Mexico.

One evening, while we were all having dinner together like we always did each night, someone knocked on the front door of our house. In those days, my mother had a lady helping with the housework. After all, she had to manage a house with four boys, my father, and my grandmother. The lady who helped in our house went to the door to inquire. She came back to the dining table and said to my mother, "It's a beggar and he says he is hungry."

We were looking from the table through the corridor leading to the entrance. We could see the man standing just outside the door. My mother, as always, never refused food to anybody who came to our house, and she put together a large plate with chicken, beef, rice, and some cheese. (My father was a cheese lover and cheeses were quite often present on the table.) My mother happily took the plate to the man and he took it. After looking over the full plate, he said to my mother in a serious, no-joke way, "You forgot the tortillas!"

For years we laughed about it in my family. Sometimes, you really cannot please some people, no matter how hard you try. But you must not let those situations ruin your sense of what is right, or your feelings of happiness about trying to do the small things that can hopefully make a difference in the world, no matter how tiny they might appear.

Go ahead and try to make a positive difference in someone's life. But remember, once in a while, you're going to find a beggar with a stick!

CHAPTER XXIII

Les Misérables

*Misery loves company, the old adage goes, and
unfortunately, it's true for a lot of people.*

Les Misérables, by Victor Hugo, is a wonderful novel. I read it many years ago, but some of its main characters I still remember, perhaps because those names became familiar again from listening to the musical of the same name.

In the novel and play, the characters have some real reasons to be unhappy. But I see so many people today who complain about how unhappy they are, even with all the blessings that surround them. It seems that even in our great land of abundance, the miserable club can always find some more members. So many people are just too quick to dwell in negativity.

Around my piano, I have quite often heard people complain that "children today are not as well behaved as in the past," or that "they don't make movies like in the old days." You get the drift. And of course, most people around the person making a statement like that usually nod in agreement. But not me. The complainers are never happy with my answers because I never do agree with those statements. When somebody starts ranting about how today's children are not as well behaved as in their youth, I try something. I tell them the following quote:

"What is happening to our young people? They disrespect their elders, they disobey their parents. They ignore the laws. They have wild notions. Their morals are decaying. What is to become of them?"

They always nod in agreement, and then I tell them the news: "You'll be surprised to learn that that statement was written by the great philosopher Plato…more than 2,000 years ago!" They usually give me a polite nod and go back to complaining to those who will listen. They usually will give me this "you don't understand" look.

I also do not agree with the claim that movies were better in the past. I sincerely think that they have always made great *and* bad movies. It was true in the past and its true today. Same goes for music.

Once you begin to subscribe to the idea of "everything in the past was better," I think you stop growing emotionally and you join the choir of "les misérables."

A modest word of advice: The next time you hear someone around you complaining about how things used to be so much better in the old days, turn around and walk away. It's not good to be trapped in their miserable way of looking at life. I am simply not in communion with that way of thinking. Turn around and walk away, because you don't want to stop growing up emotionally. Also, because I don't have issues about, as they call it today, "belonging," I think I go through life with a happier attitude.

I'll give you another typical example in my life. I remember one time in Tucson, at one of my first dinner parties in America, the guests started reminiscing about their childhoods after dinner. They were kind of going around the table, trading stories, but all they would talk about was TV.

One would say, "I grew up watching *The Lone Ranger.*" The rest would nod in agreement. The next guest would say, "I grew up watching *Lassie,*" followed by more of the same nodding. Another would mention another childhood show, with more of the "I grew up with…" type of stories, until it was my turn. I always speak the truth, so this time was no exception: "I didn't watch TV when I was growing up. We didn't have one. I grew up reading books and playing my piano."

I got some forced smiles and smirks that said "give me a break." Then they simply turned to each other and continued with their happy memories. In situations like that, I always get a feeling like I've gone to my high school reunion and realized, after an hour or so that I was at the wrong school.

When I tell that story, someone usually says "I'm sorry Antonio, I'm sure you felt like you weren't part of the group," or something along those lines. I guess it would make some people feel like an outsider.

Well, I didn't feel like I was part of that group, but it never, ever bothered me. Still today, when I have similar experiences, it doesn't bother me. See, it's another one of the great fringe benefits of not worrying about having to belong. (By the way, when I first came to America, whenever I heard that expression, I thought they were saying "French benefits," and I would always wonder why they wouldn't say "American benefits!")

You never feel like an outsider when you feel happy and content being in your own skin. You'll feel better when you stop worrying about belonging or being a part of certain groups. And you'll also feel better if you stop finding faults anywhere you can. Yes, I know that some people have a great need to belong to certain groups or be a part of a communal way of thinking, even if it's negative. If that's you, well, it's your business. But that's not me. I focus on what's good. And I am just happy being me. If you just give it a try, stay positive, and accept that your own uniqueness is one of the wonders of being a human being, you'll start to feel better about yourself and happier about life in general.

Even though misery loves company, I choose not to be a part of that company. Why would anyone choose otherwise?

CHAPTER XXIV

Peccatum Minuta

During my childhood years, if we were confronted with a problem that in my grandmother's judgment was not a big deal, she always said the Latin phrase "peccatum minuta."

Saying *peccatum minuta* was our grandmother's way of telling us not to make mountains out of molehills. Loosely translated, it means "small fault" or "minute mistake." I don't know if she was using proper Latin, but we heard that expression quite often.

My father, who was a very patient and wise man with a great love for philosophy, used to say to my brothers and me, under similar circumstances, "*Te estas ahogando en un vaso de agua,*" which means, "You are drowning yourself in a glass of water."

These two early lessons had a lasting effect on the way that I look at life. If you start trying to think in a philosophical way, you'll learn not to sweat the small stuff, and you'll probably feel more at peace, less stressed, and generally happier.

We all should learn to count our many blessings instead of worrying about trivial matters. It's also good to keep in mind the old adage "The grass is always greener on the other side of the fence." Next time you catch yourself complaining about whatever it is people so often complain about, take a couple of minutes to look around. I'm sure you'll realize that you don't have it that bad after all, and that you wouldn't want to trade places with anybody. Personally, I would never change myself for anybody else in the world. Remember, there's only one me and there's only one you.

Keep in mind that little phrase, "*peccatum minuta*." It will bring you closer to happiness when you feel like things aren't going your way. There is certainly always something to celebrate and be thankful for.

And of course, that coin has another side. Even though you shouldn't sweat the small stuff, you *should* savor and appreciate the little things in life that are good. I think that an accumulation of little happy moments can add up to a happy day. A collection of those happy days might start you on a path towards a more permanent feeling of happiness. But you can start with the little things.

For me, one of those little moments happens when I take a shower every morning. There is something special and relaxing about taking a long hot shower first thing in the morning. Even if it means I have to miss that extra 15 or 20 minutes of sleep, it's worth it.

A shower not only can help you relax, but it's also a perfect, quiet opportunity to indulge in some healthy daydreaming, planning, or fanta-sizing about your future. It's also a good time to prepare for the day ahead. In my case, during my long showers, I think about life, family, music, and my goals. Just closing my eyes and feeling the warm water is a wonderfully relaxing feeling.

Many times, I have composed songs in the shower. The only problem is that I usually have to jump out of the bath, run towards the piano, find some music notation paper and a pencil, and jot down the basics of the tune that's in my head, before it vanishes forever. After I do that, I get right back in the shower and continue to enjoy myself.

My advice to countless people to take a long shower has always gotten positive feedback, although when I first suggest it, I often hear, "I don't have the time." Then I always ask them why they don't just get up 20 minutes earlier, but most people protest that they really need their sleep.

I don't know about you, but I'm planning on taking a long nap when I am not on this earth anymore. Right now, I'm too excited living and have no time to waste being unproductive. It's just my personality, but if you train yourself to cut a bit out of your nightly sleep routine to have time for a long, relaxing shower, you'll be surprised at how much it will add to your day.

Yes, I know what you're thinking: "People don't really know how much sleep I need." Everybody says that. Maybe you do, or maybe not, but I wonder why I have heard that story so many times.

Go ahead. After this chapter, take that long shower and just *think*. It will relax you and make you feel good, and you'll have taken another step towards figuring out this business of happiness.

You shouldn't let "*peccatum minuta*" and small inconveniences slow you down. But you *should* savor the countless little pleasures of life. They tend to add up. Remember, it's the little things.

CHAPTER XXV

From Veracruz to the Beverly Hills Hotel

Years ago, while browsing in a bookstore (always one of my favorite places to hang around), I first read the following seven words, which created a lasting impression on me: "Nothing is impossible to a willing heart."

Think about it: "Nothing is impossible to a willing heart." That quote was written by John Heywood, a 16th-century English writer.

Those words made an indelible imprint on my mind because they expressed, in a simple but brilliant way, some of my own philosophical principles. I felt a sense of communion with that phrase, which so accurately defined my outlook on life.

When I think of those words, mostly I think of my career as a professional pianist. In so many ways, my willing heart has helped me find success and happiness in my music. I've mentioned my piano playing many times already, but let me tell you about how my career really began.

When I was living in Veracruz, the happy and charming place where I was born, an aunt of mine, Paz Navarro de Almazan, a piano teacher, first mentioned to my parents that the only way I could have a shot at being a pianist was to move to Mexico City and study at the National Conservatory of Music.

At first, the thought of leaving the warm security of my family was a bit disconcerting. After all, in my family, nobody left home unless they were going to get married. I remember talking about it with some friends. I encountered a phenomenon that I would come to experience all throughout life, something you also have probably experienced: the never-ending chorus of "It's too hard" and "Why complicate your life," etc., etc.

But thanks to my parents' wisdom, common sense prevailed and I moved to Mexico City. When I was introduced by my aunt to the director of the Conservatory, Professor Joaquin Amparan, I could never have imagined where my life would lead me and how different it would be from my past.

First, he asked me to play something for him. I think I played some Chopin and probably the "*Rondo Capriccioso*" by Mendelssohn. When I finished playing, he said to me: "Very well. Now I have to tell you something. Life as a pianist is very, very hard. Most students at the Conservatory never graduate, because the program is long and hard and it takes 10 years. You'll have to spend many hours practicing and forget about going to parties and having a regular, normal life. Music will be your life, and studying hard will be your everyday companion. On top of that, it's very difficult to make a living and support yourself only as a pianist. Do you still want to be a student here?"

I said, "Yes, I do," and he never talked about that subject again.

I was very lucky that day, because Professor Amparan took me in as one of his own students. As the director of the Conservatory, he was very busy and only had time and space for five or six pupils. He studied in Berlin and in Austria and had been a student of the famed Mexican composer Manuel M.

Ponce. In fact, when Ponce moved to France, the old maestro left my teacher in charge of teaching his fellow piano students.

While in Europe, my teacher also became a student of Max Pauer, who himself was a student of the great Franz Liszt. Ponce studied with the great pianist Martin Krause, Krause was a student of Liszt, Liszt studied with Carl Czerny and Czerny studied with Beethoven. By the way, Max Pauer's father, Ernest Pauer, studied piano with Mozart's son Franz Xaver Wolfgang Mozart. Professor Amparan actually had a couple of hairs from Liszt himself. I never did find out how he acquired those strands of hair from the genius composer and pianist, who's been called the greatest pianist that ever lived.

To think about that sense of history makes me feel humble and extremely lucky. After all, my teacher had a constant supply of stories, some of them from his own teacher, who knew and studied under Liszt, one of my heroes.

After a few years of studying piano and practically being a slave to music, I had a couple of disappointments in national competitions that could have changed my life forever. The only one that I won was the Frederic Chopin National Piano competition in Mexico City, but that first prize didn't have a life-changing attachment. Still, I persevered.

In those days, I would still go home for Christmas, of course. My brothers and I would sing Christmas carols for our parents. We had, and maybe they still do, a tradition in Veracruz of going around the neighboring houses singing with *la rama*, a tree branch. This old tradition entails cutting down a large tree branch and decorating it. We would put colorful, homemade paper chains around the branch, as well as some "*farolitos*" (colorful little *faroles*, or paper lanterns, with little candles in the middle), and "*sonajas*" (homemade rattles). To make the rattles, we would collect and use the tops of soda pop drinks. In those days, the drinks came in glass bottles and the top of each bottle was capped by a "*corcholata*," a cover made of tin and cork. We would take the cork material out of the cover, hit the cap with a hammer until it was flat, and then we would grab a nail and poke a hole in its center. We would then string together about 10 or so caps onto a piece of flexible wire, and voilà! We had our rattles.

Because my brothers have a great musical ear and a natural ability to learn how to sing harmonies, we were always pretty successful at going around the neighboring houses to sing and collect tips from people who would open their doors. Sometimes they'd give us candy, and on some occasions, they'd give us a little bit of cash.

On one such Christmas vacation at home, after a few years at the Conservatory and a couple of years closer to my elusive graduation as a concert pianist, I had the idea to ask my brothers, "Why don't we make a band with the four of us and move to Mexico City?"

My parents, always very supportive of all of us, moved the whole family to the big city. Once again, I heard the usual complaints: "It's so hard to find a job as a band," "You have no musical instruments," "You need managers," etc., etc.

Well, after a few rehearsals and going into debt by purchasing our instruments on credit, we got our first job playing in a very nice restaurant for their New Year's Eve party. From then on, we were very lucky to perform in the top discothèques in Mexico City, Acapulco, and some other great places.

After a few years of trying to make it with the band while I was pursuing my studies to graduate as a concert pianist, my life was extremely hectic and busy. I told my brothers that if we didn't make good progress in a year, I was going to move to the USA.

As you know, I did end up moving to America, for many reasons which could take up a whole other book. When I made the decision, once again, the chorus of negativity came into action. I heard it over and over: "It's too difficult," and "Antonio, you have no idea how difficult it is to move to the USA and work, especially as a pianist; you don't know anybody there." And on and on. But it all worked out for me, and I eventually settled here in Los Angeles. But I didn't wind up in L.A. right away.

First, as you may recall, I spent a few years in Tucson. But I also lived in Hawaii and Australia for a bit too! During this time in my life, I remember having a little argument with my then-fiancée. To cool down, I took a trip to Los Angeles to see a show, *Evita*. While in Los Angeles, I called a couple friends of mine that I had met in Honolulu. They were regular customers at the Hyatt Regency in Waikiki, where I performed while I lived in Hawaii. I was already considering what it would be like to play in Los Angeles, although at the time I thought it was a very remote possibility. I asked my friends, "Where would be a great place to play in L.A.?" And they said to me, "The Beverly Hills Hotel, the 'Home of the Stars.'" They also explained that it would be almost impossible to get a job there.

The following day, I found out the address of the "Pink Palace," as it was called then, and I went to see for myself. It was amazing, and filled with old Hollywood flavor. After all, the likes of Elizabeth Taylor, Marilyn Monroe, and Frank Sinatra used to hang around there. And Howard Hughes had a permanent suite at the hotel, which was also home to the world-famous Polo Lounge. Well, after wandering around that beautiful place for a little while, I was pretty amazed by the surroundings, to say the least.

Walking through the hotel, I asked where the office of the general manager was. Soon enough, I found myself sitting there in his small reception room outside his private office. I think his secretary thought that I had an appointment, which I didn't, and she told me, "Mr. Richman will be back in a few minutes."

Eventually, Jordan Richman, the general manager of the Beverly Hills Hotel at the time, if my memory doesn't fail me, walked in, shook my hand, and asked me to come into his office. After a quick introduction, he asked me if I had an appointment, because he didn't know me.

I said to him, "I don't know you. My name is Antonio Castillo de la Gala. I am a pianist and one day I would love to play in your hotel." He gave me a strange look and explained nicely that they already had a pianist. Actually, he explained that they had two. Well, I had nothing to lose at that point. So, I said to him, "But you haven't heard anything yet." He gave me another quizzical look and then made a phone call to have the banquet manager, the head chef, and the maitre d' meet with him at the Cotterie (the elegant restaurant at the hotel in those days). He said on the phone, "I have a guy here who thinks he's a good pianist."

So, we went down to the restaurant together and I played a couple of songs. After I finished, I was thinking that maybe I would send him a tape from Tucson, along with my résumé, and leave my business card with him there. I thought that maybe one day I would get that lucky call.

I'll never forget what Mr. Richman said next: "When would you like to start at the Beverly Hills Hotel?" How about that? I asked him for a couple of weeks to be able to put my things in order in Tucson and give notice to the restaurant where I was performing at the time, and I told him I'd be back after that.

"Nothing is impossible to a willing heart."

When I went back to Tucson, nobody believed my story, and every time that I said I was moving to L.A. to be the pianist at the Beverly Hills Hotel, I just received more looks of bewilderment and polite smiles.

I can't say that I blame them for their disbelief. After all, the day before I went to the Beverly Hills Hotel, a friend of mine who lived in Southern California had taken me to her favorite place, the Hotel Bel-Air, and introduced me to the resident pianist there. After a casual hello, he said to me, "You better stay in Tucson. The odds of getting a job as a pianist in Los Angeles, especially at a fine hotel, are one in a million."

That pianist has since moved on to the next life. I wonder sometimes if he is smiling up there, or wherever he is, because, as I've mentioned before,

I was the resident pianist at the world-famous Hotel Bel-Air for more than 12 years. What can I say?

Somebody once wrote an article about me in a Tucson magazine with the title "One Shot in a Million." I guess you could say that I'm lucky, but I don't think that it is all luck. It also comes down to having a good attitude, being positive, and trying to make things happen.

Just remember that quote: "Nothing is impossible to a willing heart." If I can do it, after coming from Mexico with no connections, friends, or relatives, with hardly any knowledge of English, and with only a couple of suitcases and a pocket full of dreams, then you can do it to.

I came here with dreams of a career and my desire to always search out happiness. Attaining happiness takes some planning. You need to first eliminate the negative thoughts of "You can't do it" and "It's too hard" from your mind. Then the rest becomes that much easier. "Nothing is impossible to a willing heart."

CHAPTER XXVI

Motivation and the Next Mountain

Motivation is the fuel that will enable
you to bring your dreams to life.

Finding motivation is the difficult part. It should be in every facet of your life, and yet you should still always be pursuing more. In your career goals and even in your search for happiness, motivation is the factor that will bring you to success. As has happened so many times in my life, this lesson came to me from the most unexpected of places.

In 1980, I was playing piano at Charles Restaurant, which was at that time a very elegant place in Tucson, Arizona. In those days, you never knew who might walk into that restaurant. One night, I had the pleasure to meet the great entertainer Liberace. He had dinner there and then walked into the lounge where I was playing. His comments about my piano playing were very gracious.

Liberace was doing a show in the city and I was invited the following day to a reception in his honor. We had our picture taken together that night and it was a very special moment. I was also fortunate to see his show in

Las Vegas, and he put on an amazing display of showmanship of the highest caliber.

After my brief conversation with Liberace and after watching his show, one thing was clear: he was a man trying to spread happiness to everyone around him, a very positive human being. I have been fortunate in meeting many people who were close to him on a personal and professional level, and I have consistently been told of his great kindness. I think he positively influenced the lives of millions of fans around the world. And I believe that spreading joy was his main motivation.

A few years ago, I had the pleasure to play his fantastic pianos at the Liberace Museum in Las Vegas. I even got to play a concert on one that had also been owned once by George Gershwin. It was a great thrill, just like our meeting. I understand that, unfortunately, as of these writings, the museum is closed.

On a different night, the restaurant hosted a private dinner honoring the distinguished Dr. Christiaan Barnard, who in 1967 found a place for himself in the history and medical books by performing the first successful human heart transplant, in South Africa. At the dinner, the famous surgeon gave a very amusing speech. Then he came to my piano and sat right down next to me!

You can imagine my surprise at seeing a distinguished individual such as Dr. Barnard sitting with me at my piano. When he sat down, he introduced himself (as if it were necessary) and asked about me, my life, and my training. Can you believe it? Here he was, at a dinner in his honor, and he was interviewing the pianist. He complimented my playing and then made a few song requests, which I happily played for him, of course. I remember how eclectic they were: Chopin, the *Warsaw Concerto*, "The Entertainer." What a great guy.

As always happens when I am in the presence of someone who has made a real difference in the quality of people's lives, I was in awe and I wanted to ask him so many questions while we were talking. One in particular came to mind: I asked him how he could top himself after having performed that amazing feat of the first successful human heart transplant and securing his place in history. I asked him what kept him motivated to try to achieve more in his life.

He thought for a couple of seconds and said to me, "Yes, doing that first operation was like climbing a big mountain, but when I came down from that mountain, I saw the next one."

Those words of wisdom stayed with me and are imbedded in my memory. I took that personal lesson to heart, and once in a while, when I am having trouble finding the motivation to make that next step or put in that extra effort to try to make a difference in the world and in the lives of the people around me, I think about Dr. Barnard and his wise words.

I think this is definitely relevant to the pursuit of happiness. Always try to climb that next personal mountain in your life. Always stay motivated to do better.

When I speak with other musicians and they tell me how "lucky" I am to always have permanent jobs playing the piano and how it is so difficult to get a break in this country, I tell them about my own experience. When I came to the USA and tried to have a career as a professional pianist, it was the equivalent to coming to the plate at a baseball game with already 2 strikes. Every day. Or play a game of tennis where every time I started the match, I would be already losing 0-5 and 0-fourty. No room for mistakes. I always ask them if it was hard to get papers to become a permanent resident or a citizen, they always say "No, I was born here". When I mention if they had to study a lot to be fluent in English and if they had to walk always with a English-Spanish Dictionary, they always tell me "No, English is my mother language". When I tell them that I didn't have one single friend, parent, sibling or relative in this country, what was their situation? They always tell me that they had parents, siblings, friends, teachers, etc. Then, some of them understand that it wasn't easy or I was "lucky" to try to have a career in this country. The harder I worked, the "luckier" I was.

Motivation was a strong factor in to having a better life in the USA, another tool to my pursuit of happiness.

CHAPTER XXVII

"How Do I Get to Hollywood?"

We've all heard about the power of positive thinking. But I think it's more than just a catchy phrase, and people sometimes underestimate just how real the concept is.

I have experienced, over and over, how having a positive attitude towards life can yield great responses. As I've mentioned before, the "It's really hard, you have no chance" crowd can be very influential in people's lives and decisions, and they can have detrimental effects on your finding happiness.

This reminds me of one of my favorite stories. When I was still very new to the United States and starting out in Tucson, one of the aspects of American life that really grabbed my attention was the game show phenomenon on TV. Watching those contestants winning prizes was quite exciting and new for me. One day, I found myself watching a game show called *Card Sharks* with a lovely lady who I was dating at the time. I said to her, "I bet you and I can do that, it looks very easy." She laughed and said to me, "Antonio, you are not even American, you just got into the U.S., and your English is not that great yet, so forget about it. The odds of you making it on a national game show aren't very good."

A couple of days later, she even brought some information on odds that she found at the University of Arizona, where she was a student. She proceeded to tell me about the odds of being hit by lightning, of winning the lottery, of being on a national game show, etc. I think that the odds of being on a game show were around 200,000 to one.

Still, I said to her, "I'll be on a game show, you'll see."

A couple of weeks later, I asked the maitre d' of the restaurant where I was working, "Charles, how do I get to Hollywood?" He gave the same funny look I always seem to get from people, smiled, and then grabbed the map that I had brought with me. With a pencil, he proceeded to draw a line from Tucson, Arizona, straight to Los Angeles, California. He said, "Take Route 10 West and you'll be in Hollywood." I left his office and that very Sunday I got in my car with the map and I took off for L.A.

When I arrived in the Los Angeles area, I realized that I had absolutely no idea how to get to Hollywood. All I could do was drive around and try to find my own way. Fortunately, I ended up catching a glimpse of the big Hollywood sign and stopped in that area to ask questions. Then I checked into a hotel and immediately asked the front desk about the TV studios where they filmed *Card Sharks*. They gave me the address, and Monday morning I was in the parking lot of the studio.

I looked at the directory at the entrance and I took the elevator to the offices with the name *Card Sharks* on it. I walked into a busy room with a lot of people, and the receptionist said to me, "Hi, may I help you?" I announced, "I am here because I want to be on *Card Sharks*."

She asked me my name, and after checking the paper in front of her, she told me that I wasn't on the list for that day's auditions. Uh-oh…the word "auditions" had a funny sound to me. But I pressed on and explained to her the truth, that I didn't have an appointment. She asked me, "Did you send a postcard? Did you call for an audition date?" I told her, "No, I watched the show in Tucson, where I live, drove here yesterday in my car, and here I am." I said this with my best Sunday smile.

I think she got a kick out of me because she said, "You mean to tell me that you drove here from Tucson, had no appointment, we didn't call you, you didn't write to us, you just showed up here, and now you want to be on the show?" I said yes, that's exactly what I did and what I wanted. She then turned and talked to somebody else and said to me, "Come in and wait in that chair. We'll take your picture."

To make a long story short, all the applicants were divided into three different groups, with each group made up of more than a hundred people. At the end of the day, they chose one person: me.

You can probably imagine the looks of surprise I got when I went back to Tucson and everybody saw me on *Card Sharks*. My girlfriend was the most surprised of all.

It was so much fun that I eventually decided it would be great to be on the show another time. When the night edition of *Card Sharks* went on the air, I tried again. This time, though, I called. I auditioned. And I did it. Again. I was on *Card Sharks* a second time. I even won a great trip to Brazil, compliments of the show.

So, what were the odds of me being on a national game show twice? They weren't that great, that's for sure. To be on a third nationally televised game show, the odds must be off the charts. But I did it. I was on *Family Feud*!

Just think of that old phrase I like: "Nothing is impossible to a willing heart." The power of positive thinking is remarkable.

Is being on a TV show a recipe for happiness? Of course not, but the idea of the power of positive thinking is real and tangible to me. And, as I said before, I think that the happier moments you add to your memory bank, the happier you will be in general. For me, it wasn't about being on TV; it was about having a good time and making things happen. It was about making more deposits to my memory bank. It was about the power of positive thinking.

CHAPTER XXVIII

Giving Is Happiness: A Christmas Story and Other Tales of Kindness

*If you give tortillas to life, you'll
get back enchiladas.*

To express my next point, I'm going to talk again about one of my very favorite subjects: Christmas. I told you I love Christmas! You see, some of my fondest memories are from Christmases in my past. Here is one such story.

While I was playing at Macy's Plaza, they used to have — and I hope that they still do — a Christmas tree with written notes hanging all over it. The notes were from children of all ages, and they each had a request for a Christmas present: "Susan, age 10: I would love a doll and a book for Christmas. Thank you for your help."

Every year it was a great joy for me to go to that tree, pick out a name, and go shopping for that little girl or boy's wish. I would get the present and bring it back, and the child would get his or her gift.

One particular year, my financial status was not in great shape (nothing new for a professional pianist). I remember going to see that Christmas tree and looking at all of the names and reading their wishes. I realized that I didn't have enough cash and that my credit cards were at the max, so I walked away and headed for the bookstore. I loved to browse in that bookstore, and I would often go in there before I went home after I was done performing.

While I was in the bookstore that day, I somehow drifted towards the children's books. All of a sudden, I felt a tremendous feeling of sadness and I started to cry. Feeling embarrassed, I hid my face in a book and waited until the feeling passed.

I knew what was making me sad. I couldn't stop thinking about a card that I had just read from a girl who wanted a book for Christmas. Feeling really bad about myself, I reached into my pockets. I had about $22.00. I went to find her book and bought it. Then I brought it back to Macy's to give it to one of the ladies in charge of that Christmas tree. Let me tell you, I walked out of that mall feeling like a million dollars. I was happy again, the way I like to feel.

This was the beginning of my Christmas story.

On my way to the office where I would change from my tuxedo into my street clothes, a lady stopped me and said, "I am so glad I found you, because I asked around and they told me that you finished at two and I was sure that you were gone. We need a pianist for a last-minute party for our office tomorrow, and if I didn't find you today, we were going to call an agency so they could provide one."

I agreed to play at the party the following day and I thought to myself: "My God, if I had gone home instead of shopping for that little girl, I would have missed this opportunity to make some much-needed extra money."

Next, before going to change clothes, I decided to walk to the counter in the mall where they sold lottery tickets and I bought a scratch-off ticket for one dollar. A foolish move, I know, since all I had left on me at the time was about three dollars. Still, I spent my one dollar and scratched the ticket. That was the first and only time in my life, up to that moment, that I had a $50 winner.

Those 50 dollars really came in handy, and I couldn't help but think about almost missing the opportunity. I became even happier that I had bought the book for that little girl. But that's not the end of my Christmas story.

That night, I was playing at the Polo Lounge at the Beverly Hills Hotel. Just after I closed my piano for the night, a waiter approached me and pointed to a couple who had just come in late for a bite to eat. They had requested that I play "just a couple of songs."

I went back to open the piano and I played a few songs. It turns out that the man was Tom Berenger, the famous actor. When I was finished playing, he very graciously said to me, "Thank you for staying longer and playing for us." When he shook my hand, he handed me a crisp $50 bill.

Well, after that, I was feeling even happier and I was ready to go home. On the way to my car in the parking lot, I was talking out loud, as I often do. I was recalling all of my reasons to be grateful that day, and I thanked God for all the many blessings in my life. Right then, in the middle of the parking lot, I looked down to see a $10 bill. I picked it up and had a big smile.

Coincidence? It's up to you to decide.

Of course, Christmas isn't the only time to give to other people and to offer kindness. Another cute story happened with me and a friend who I have known for many years. Every once in a while, we would get together to have an ice-blended mocha and a cookie.

They used to have this great cookie place in the mall. During my breaks from work, I would enjoy my ice-cold drink and read a book. Then I would stop and buy a sugar cookie from the cookie store. They had the best sugar cookies that I ever tasted.

I always noticed that the majority of customers would just point to the cookies, say which ones they wanted and how many, and then leave the counter without even acknowledging the presence of the person on the other side. I don't do it to be cute or anything, but I was raised to say hello and be polite with everybody, so I always ask people how they're doing, how their day is going. I did the same thing with the cookie person behind the counter whenever I would buy my cookie. Quite often, when I got to my table, I would notice that I had an extra cookie in my bag.

One particular day, I met a friend at the mall. After getting our ice-blended drinks, we headed towards the cookie place.

When we got there, my friend pointed to one of the chocolate-chip cookies and said, "I'll have one of those, please." Then the guy behind the counter looked at me and said, "What would you like, Antonio?" (I always like to introduce myself where I do business often, so he knew my name). I told him that I would also like a chocolate-chip cookie. He said, "Let me get you a warm one, just fresh from the oven."

You should have seen the bewildered look on my friend's face. I paid and we walked towards a table. She was fuming in a kind of a half-joking way. "I can't believe it!" she said. "What do you have that I don't? Is it just because you speak Spanish?" She was livid and I was smiling.

I said to her that I always make a point to have a conversation and ask about the person's day. She is a very polite lady and a successful business-woman, but I guess she probably hadn't ever thought about it.

The point of the story is that just by taking a few seconds to take an interest in other people's feelings, you can make them feel good. Whether they're across the counter at the bank, the post office, or your favorite cookie store, or if it's just someone you run into throughout the course of your day, be kind to them and treat them with respect. Being nice to everybody creates smoother relationships and will always make people smile.

Take my small example. I became friends with the cookie people, and they would do nice things like give me extra cookies. To me, a wonderfully happy moment is when I can read a book and enjoy a warm, fresh-from-the-oven chocolate-chip cookie along with an ice-cold glass of milk (or blended mocha). And it helps to know that I was nice to other people and helped them be happier too.

Yes, we all know the meaning of kindness. Our parents told us over and over to be kind to one another. Perhaps we don't heed that advice often enough, but when we do, the results are wonderful.

Indeed, I think that being kind is one of the best gifts you can give to others. Here's another example. When I was playing at Macy's Plaza among the thousands of customers that came by my piano throughout all those years, the same situation would often unfold in front of me. A businessman, a big-time manager in one of the business offices in the building, would come down once in a while to enjoy his lunch by my piano. He would make a couple of requests, thank me, and then go back to work.

Eventually, I met his secretary. She told me that she could always tell when her boss had had lunch by my piano rather than at his usual business meetings, because he would always be nicer to her afterwards. She said that after hearing the music, he would come back to the office with a smile on his face. The fact that I played a part in making him act nicer made me feel good.

As if that weren't enough, I actually met the wife of that same businessman on another occasion. The first words that she said to me were: "My husband speaks wonderfully of your playing. I wish that he would come down to have lunch while listening to your piano more often. Whenever he listens to you, he comes home nicer and calmer. Even our kids can always tell the difference."

You can just imagine the amazing snowball effect of that situation. If the secretary was feeling better after her boss was nicer to her, then she would probably be in a better mood when she got home. Then that mood would reflect in a positive manner on her family. The same goes for the businessman, when he got home and was nicer to his wife and kids, they would probably feel better, and then they'd be nicer too. For me, all I had to do was play his favorite songs and perhaps listen to his story for a bit to make him smile. And seeing him smile would make me happy. Just picture the multiplying effect. I would give the gift of music and be kind. He would feel happier and be kinder to the people around him. And so on, and so on. That's the power of kindness.

You really can't overestimate what kindness can do for people. Try being kinder than usual to the people around you. You'll probably feel the effects right away. It will make you feel happier and you'll make other people happy as well.

And of course, think of those little children at Christmastime. I can't begin to express how happy it made me feel to help bring just a little joy into their lives. And once you start giving, life will start to give you back even more. The power of giving is an amazing thing: it makes someone else happy, but believe me, it will make you much happier too.

In his play *Candida*, George Bernard Shaw wrote, "We have no more right to consume happiness without producing it than to consume wealth without producing it."

You see? Sometimes when you give life a tortilla, it will come back as an enchilada.

CHAPTER XXIX

To Date or Not to Date...

If you're someone who believes that being in a relationship is paramount to making you feel happy, then by all means this chapter is for you.

Well, I guess it would be hard to write a book about happiness without talking about relationships and love. It's a very complicated subject, but of course it's a crucial part of happiness. I think I have some helpful insights.

Sitting at my piano all these years and playing music for people has given me the precious and probably unique opportunity to watch couples, thousands of couples. After all this time, watching behavior between the sexes is like reading an open book for me.

By observing the people around my piano — truly thousands of couples and single people throughout the years — I have learned how to be able to tell, almost with 100% accuracy, the kind of relationship that they have. Sometimes just by reading their faces I can tell who is married, who is cheating, who has been married too long, who is having a first date, who is trying hard but getting nowhere, who is hitting it off, who is not, who is having an anniversary, etc., etc.

Quite often, to test my "readings," I approach the couple. By having a short conversation, I can usually find out the truth. I come away reassured that my perception of their particular situation was correct almost every time. It's almost as if I know how their own particular love story will end before they do. I've seen it all so many times.

Ah, the dating game. I have gained a clearer perspective on relationships not only by observing and talking to thousands of couples, but also through spending many years in the dating world myself. As my father used to say, "If I tell you that the donkey is brown, it's because I'm holding brown donkey's hairs in my hands." In other words, I know from experience. On top of that, probably because music tends to relax people and give them a temporary sense of peace, people often let their guards down around me. As a result, I have heard the stories of countless couples.

The lounge of a fine hotel is an ideal scenario where these nightly plays are performed, and usually I am, besides being the pianist and provider of the soundtrack, an ardent and happy audience of one. The cornucopia of situations is unbelievable, but listening to all those stories has given me a unique and clear perspective on how men and women relate to one another. Of course, I can't go into too much detail here about dating. After all, with the number of stories I have heard, I could easily write another book! Instead, I will focus on two of the main problems I have encountered, the first being some advice for women and the second for men, in the hopes of perhaps helping you along on the road to happiness and love.

Ladies first.

I happen to have many lady friends — casual acquaintances, regular customers of the hotel, piano students, friends, and former girlfriends — and they all seem to share something in common. In so many words, they ask me, "Antonio, why is it so hard to find a man who is sensitive, one who dresses well, loves to listen, enjoys going shopping and seeing *Phantom of the Opera*, takes care of his body, has a sense of style, and knows how to treat a lady well?"

My standard answer is, "I know many guys like that, but they all have boyfriends." After the laughter subsides, I try to teach them the red flags to look out for when meeting men. And there are many — you just have to pay attention. But there is one in particular that I will talk about here.

I've had plenty of firsthand experience in situations where a lady friend of mine has just found a new boyfriend. They will often call me up and say, "I just met this guy and I am going to bring him to the hotel so that you can give me your opinion."

Due to my unwavering optimism, I will always wish them the best. But the close friends who know me well will say, "I know that you are always positive, but please, just tell me your honest thoughts after you meet this guy."

There are many types of guys who approach women in a variety of ways. We can try to narrow that list to some general types that are easy to recognize, including the guys who play the "game" the best. You see, the main thing I think ladies need to watch out for is the insincere guys. You know the type: they're the guys who lay it on thick, but they're fake. They're sometimes referred to as "players."

The player is the number-one master of the dating game. He is the guy who plays the "I'm going to die if you are not with me" card. Have you seen them in the movies? The usual story is that a guy meets a girl, they start dating, and then they have a fight. That same night, usually a rainy night, he'll be under her window screaming her name, yelling, "I love you! Please forgive me, I can't live without you." And of course, a sad song from the latest teenage sensation will be playing in the background.

Of course, you know that by the end of the movie, she'll forgive him and they will have a happy ending. Well, variations of that same drama play out every night in lounges and bars all over America.

Let me give you an example of how this guy behaves. A couple will come into the lounge. If I know the guy, he'll introduce me to his new date. I'll introduce myself and ask how they met each other, and he'll say something like, "I'm so lucky, I've been trying to ask her out for weeks and she finally said yes." One such gentleman, who has brought more than 100 girls to the lounge where I work, always says to me, "We're getting married next week."

Well, the lady will often look a bit embarrassed, but slightly flattered by the attention. When they're back to their table and ordering their food, the player will say, "Whatever you want honey, the desserts are great here."

She'll pick out a dessert and then he'll take her hand. Then he'll usually start by saying how tiny and pretty her hands are compared to his. It's an old trick, but it always works. Then he might say something like, "You have nice, long, delicate fingers; do you play the piano?" Not long after that initial touch, they will be holding hands.

Next, the dessert arrives.

He'll ignore it because he is really into her. He'll have eyes like a lamb going to the butcher — sad, droopy eyes. He might try to rest his head on her shoulder and make her believe that nothing else matters in the world but her.

If the player plays the game well — and some of those guys are truly experts — she'll slowly start feeding him the crème brûlée. Once in a while he'll refuse because he doesn't want to "break the special moment," as I have heard countless times. The girl will feel warm all over because she thinks he is truly paying attention to her. The real expert won't even move his head from her shoulder or pay any attention to the food or drinks. Then she'll go to the bathroom to freshen up.

That's when the guy usually will come up to my piano and make some kind of comment to me in a very animated way, like, "Wow, isn't she hot?" or "I hope I get lucky!" or something along those lines.

He'll be back in his chair before she returns and, as if by magic, the nostalgic, hopeful, sad, dreamy look in his eyes is back. Just like that. And she'll believe him — most of the time, it works. The next date that he brings to the hotel will be played the same way, sometimes word for word. It's amazing.

To me, it's always obvious when this type of guy isn't being sincere. But I guess some women have such high hopes for meeting someone special that they'll miss those red flags.

There are other types too that I've seen countless times. Like the producer. There are probably thousands of "producers" around. Then there's the actor; the rich guy who never stops talking about his worldly possessions; the "I just haven't found the right woman for my lifestyle" guy; etc., etc. Next time you have a first date, just watch for those signs and you'll be in better shape to deal with them. It could save you future heartache. But especially watch out for players.

Then there's the other side of the coin.

Gentlemen, if you want to find a girlfriend, and a really meaningful relationship, then maybe I can help you. There's one scenario that I see happen over and over to guys. Maybe it's happened to you; if not, you're lucky, but you should still watch out for it.

Say you meet a nice girl. Maybe you met her at the office, or waiting in line to buy your eight-dollar cup of coffee, or at the bank, or at the supermarket, or in school. It doesn't matter. After you sweat for a while, you muster the courage to ask for her number. She gives it to you. Soon you're dreaming of your first date. But be careful: watch out for the red flags.

If you call her on a Wednesday to go out on Saturday night and she says, "Sounds good, but…call me back Friday and we'll talk again," that's a red flag. The translation is, "I'm not too crazy about going out with you. I think that I might have a better option before the end of the week. I better hold off just in case someone better (better looking, better dressed, better *anything*) comes my way. But if nobody calls by the time you call on Friday, then we'll go out, because I guess it will be better than staying home."

Do you think I'm exaggerating? No way, Jose. I have heard the truth from girls talking together in the lounge. I have heard those stories from them, straight from the horse's mouth, many, many times.

It's just a game, and you have to know the rules. Otherwise you're going to be stuck on the bench not participating or you will easily become very frustrated.

Sometimes you'll go out after the first try and then quickly set a second date and go out again. She is pretty, smart, has a sense of humor, and things are looking good. You're thinking, "I finally found myself a girlfriend!"

By the third date you try to hold her hand and…nothing. I see it all the time. She will slowly move her hand away from your anxious hand and then you'll get one of "The Speeches." Most guys will recognize when they're getting one of these speeches, but other guys are just a bit too hopeful or too blind to see what's happening.

I'll break them down for you.

Remember, I speak from personal experience and I have heard similar stories from other guys, many times over. Right when she moves her hand away, prepare yourself for the most common speech: "You know, (put your own name here), I really, really like you, and you're a *very nice guy* (the kiss of death!), but…." I'm sure you can guess the rest. It's usually some excuse like, "It's the wrong time in my life," or "I'm not ready for romance right now," or "I really value your friendship and I wouldn't want to jeopardize it." Translation: "I wouldn't sleep with you even if you were the last man on the face of the earth."

Then there are the other most common speeches: "I am too busy with my…"

a) Career

b) Life

c) Kids

d) Education

e) Plans for the future

g) Parents

You get the idea. If you listen carefully instead of dreaming about the opposite circumstances, you'll save yourself time, money, and disappointment. You'll see right off the bat that she is not interested in you romantically, and this will help you move on before you get hurt.

That is, of course, unless you already fell in love with a girl who doesn't like you back. Now you're in trouble. Big trouble.

We've all been in that boat and it's not fun. It can make you feel miserable. There are only a couple of things that I think work.

I find that it helps to visualize a perfect, warm, cozy room while I do my meditations, daydreaming, or introspective thinking. That room has the most comfortable chair that you could ever sit on, and it's the perfect temperature. It's filled with my favorite things. In my case, these are my books and my piano, but think of whatever makes you feel comfortable and happy. If you imagine yourself in that room in the middle of a hectic day or on a night when it's hard to fall asleep, you might find some solace. And this cozy room can come in very handy when you're trying to forget an unrequited love.

If you fall in love with a pretty, charming, intelligent girl and she gives you the "nice guy" speech, the game is over. You'll be better off cutting your losses and moving on.

But maybe you can't. Sometimes it is easier said than done. Maybe you think, wrongly, that she'll change her mind because she will see how nice of a guy you are. Don't kid yourself or get your hopes too high, because she probably won't.

Before you fall deeper into that hopeless love, go to your imaginary room, sit down in the cozy chair, and relax, looking out through your window to the lovely landscape outside. Imagine the vivid shapes and colors of the grass, the trees, the soft clouds, the birds flying by. Smell the flowers that are all around: a soft breeze just brought their bouquet to you.

After you are deep in that thought, now walk to your imaginary window. Imagine that you are writing that girl's name on a piece of paper. Poke your head outside the window and throw that paper away. Then close the window. Leave the room. Go on with your life. After a few tries, you'll feel better and you'll be ready to find a more realistic love.

Many guys (and girls), if they have a very healthy attitude, can maintain a friendship with the other person even after they get the speech. If that's the case, then good for you. Now everybody's happy.

As I said, I could write a whole other book on this topic, but those are the main aspects of the game of love. Everybody plays the game on different levels. Try to pay attention and you might have a little edge. Just be sure to keep your heart open and love will find you. I wish you luck!

CHAPTER XXX
Silence Is Golden

George Eliot wrote, "Blessed is the man who, having nothing to say, abstains from giving in words evidence of the fact."

We've all heard the expression "Silence is golden," but I wonder if we really grasp the meaning of the phrase. Silence is one of the pathways to happiness, in my opinion. And I'm a pianist! But allow me to explain.

Probably one of the reasons that so many people have told me their problems throughout the years is because I enjoy listening. Just listening. When somebody is telling me their troubles, I just listen without interrupting. At the end of the conversation, I'm used to hearing, "Thanks Antonio, that was very nice of you," or, one of my absolute favorites: "Thanks for the help, Antonio."

Usually I don't even really do anything. I just remain silent and listen to what they have to say. All I do is nod and really look into the person's eyes and *pay attention*. Very often, just through talking it out, people come up with their own answers to their questions or tribulations. I guess a friendly ear is often all somebody needs, but that can be very hard to find sometimes in life.

So, try listening to people instead of thinking what to say next. For guys, there may even be some fringe benefits with the ladies if you become a truly good listener.

Many, many times, I've gotten a date with a lady friend just because I was nice enough to listen to her when that's what she needed most. I can listen for hours and they truly appreciate the gesture. Sometimes, to my utter amazement, they will even respond by being very loving and warm towards me, just for listening.

I have often said to guys, "If you want to have a shot at seeing the girl again after that first date, listen, just listen. Don't try to impress her, it never works." After they tried listening, some of my guy friends have come back to tell me I was right.

It takes discipline though, because we all want to express our points of view. Still, remember that there will be plenty of time for that on the next date and the next, if you're lucky enough to get another one.

Silence is a truly great commodity in today's world. I think that it is very, very hard to find silence in our busy lives. In fact, I do a lot of my writing, musical or the other kind, mostly very late at night, because that's when it's quietest. At that time, the sounds of the city are less prominent, though they're still there.

When I go to get my daily ice-blended green tea or mocha and enjoy one of my books on my break, which offers me a great little oasis in the middle of my busy schedule, one of the hardest things to get used to is the fact that there aren't any public places that don't have piped music playing. There's simply no place that will allow silence to exist.

I have never been in a mall, shopping center, coffee place or store without music. Most of the time it makes me want to get out of there as fast as I can, but I think it might bother me more than most people. How ironic, a professional musician annoyed by music! But I get annoyed because it isn't good music. It's simply filler. It's just my opinion and personal taste.

During my years playing at fine restaurants, I noticed the same phenomenon. I always found it curious that when I would take a 10-minute break, one of the waiters would always go running to the sound system to play the piped music. I would ask the waiter, "Why do you put on that music if I'm going to return to my piano in a few minutes?" I always got the same answer: "I just can't stand silence!"

I have noticed throughout the years that when couples walk into a hotel lounge, restaurant, or bar and the maitre d' leads them to a quiet section of the establishment, they'll request, almost every time, a table closer to where "everybody else" is sitting. Me? I'm the opposite. I love to sit in the quietest section of a restaurant.

I love seeking out quiet, secluded places. A few years ago, when I was playing in Hawaii, one of the many thrilling parts about being there was the fact that you could get away from Honolulu and escape to parts of the island that were hardly developed or populated. There, you could truly find some peace and quiet. Only the sounds of the natural surroundings were in the air. What a wonderful and precious feeling.

Silence, whenever I can find it, is a very welcome commodity. It allows me to get in touch with my personal thoughts. It helps me reflect on my life and on my role on this earth.

I think that many conflicts or stressful times could be alleviated by being silent in the midst of all the chaos. I've tried it many times and it works for me. It also tends to calm the people around you. Calm is good.

So, try listening for a change. Try appreciating a quiet place where you can be alone with your thoughts. Silence can be a close, quiet friend on your journey towards being happy.

CHAPTER XXXI

Happy Holidays and All That Jazz

*We've all heard the old Chinese saying
"A thousand-mile journey begins with
the first step." I hope that you'll take
that first step today, not tomorrow.*

I think that every day can be a holiday. Personally, I've never liked the phrase "Happy Holidays," which I've heard so many times over the years. I never know which holiday they're talking about! But you can choose to make every day a holiday. Make each day a celebration of life.

Shakespeare wrote that "All the world's a stage," and you can choose between being on that stage (a doer, living, loving, enjoying, suffering, trying,) or in the audience — a spectator who merely observes life being lived by others. Every time I read how many hours people spend in front of the TV, I think about how they are not really living life. They're just watching somebody else's.

I hope that you aren't someone who wastes away in front of the TV set. Don't get me wrong, I enjoy TV as much as anybody else. It's a great way to keep myself entertained while I'm on the treadmill. It makes the time fly right by and allows me to catch up on world news. Besides the news programs, I also love arts programs, sports, 60 Minutes, Dr. Phil, Judge Judy, the Discovery Channel, and the History Channel. I'll also occasionally watch an old movie on the tube. TV is great and it can help you forget about your troubles for a little while, but, like I have said before, everything in moderation. I would never want to waste my life in front of the TV.

Obviously, I don't think I'm the only one who feels this way. But take it from Ken Farnsworth, the son of Philo Farnsworth, the inventor of the television. In a discussion about how people watch TV for hour after hour every day, he commented that they "waste a lot of their lives." This from the son of the man who *invented television itself!*

So yes, TV makes me happy sometimes, but I don't depend on it and I don't watch it all the time. Too much can keep you from actually living your life. How can each day be a holiday if you're stuck on the couch? How can you get any closer to feeling happy if you're not experiencing the joys of life?

It's just like ice cream: I love ice cream. A lot. It makes me happy. But if you eat too much, you'll have to shop for clothes way too often.

So many things make me happy in life, even the simplest things that many people take for granted. Take sleep, for example. I love crawling into my nice bed for a good night's rest. I try not to bring my stresses to bed, and it usually takes me only about five minutes to fall asleep. After I turn out the lights and close my eyes, my routine is quite simple: I say my daily prayers, give thanks for all the blessings of my day, my never-ending gratefulness and then I do some positive reinforcement. I think about my goals for the next day and life in general. Before I know it, I'm off to dreamland.

Once in a while, especially before a concert, recital, recording session, or special event or show, the music keeps playing nonstop in my head and my mind goes over the songs again and again. Occasionally this affects my sleep, and it can be very annoying, despite my great passion for music. But I guess it's a small price to pay for the joys that eventually follow. When this happens, I try to think how happy I will be to get to play music for other people. I think of how lucky I am, and I try to be grateful that I will get to add another happy moment to my memory bank.

What are the things that make you happy? I bet some of them are pretty simple. Focus on them. Try not to take them for granted. And when you are worried or agitated, keep those happy thoughts in mind. They'll make you feel better. The dividends will be amazing.

I think that feeling happy can also help you be healthier and probably even look younger. Whenever I go to Las Vegas, I try to stop at the games at one of the big hotels there. Sometimes they'll have a guy wearing a wizard outfit who will try to guess your age. These "wizards" have a huge advantage in the odds (of course) because they only have to guess within five years older or younger than your real age, and so they usually win. It's another very clever game for the house. If, for example, you're a young person in your 20s, all the wizard has to say is 25. That ensures that he will win if you are anywhere between 20 and 30 years old. Sounds like the wizards would always win, right? Well, in all the years that I've played that game, those clever wizards never guessed my age correctly. In fact, they're usually off by 15 to 25 years! Yes, a few times I even had to show my driver's license as proof.

You see, it pays to feel happy. I feel and look healthier. When I win that game, I walk away with a prize, which I usually end up giving away to a kid in the hotel. But those prizes don't matter: the real prize is that I feel better and happier. Remember that every day counts, and that every day can be a holiday. Remember the little things that make you feel better, and savor them. And get off that couch!

Some Closing Thoughts on This Business of Happiness

My father used to say to us, "Patience is a virtue." In these busy times, I have to remind myself of that phrase quite often.

In this day and age, we are all constantly bombarded with information. It can all be quite hectic and it makes it hard to think sometimes. The influence the media has in shaping our perception of life and sense of what's right and wrong is extremely strong. It's a constant battle, and I'm sure too many lives are influenced heavily by celebrities. Why do we pay attention to these people?

Not too long ago, I read an interview in a "men's magazine" with a very well-known young actor. I couldn't believe some of the things he said. When he was telling the stories of his youth, he mentioned being arrested for drunk driving, "dabbling" in a couple of illegal substances, stealing a couple cans of soda, etc. He called this behavior "typical clichéd growing-up things." Typical? Clichéd? Where? How? I felt like screaming at the guy. Call me a prude or traditional, but none of my friends and family in my hometown in

Mexico were ever arrested and they didn't behave that way. And if they had, it would *not* have been OK.

I wonder if reading those kinds of statements can influence a young person's mind, and if he might begin to consider or condone certain decisions or behaviors that could hurt his future. Maybe too many people have the "if a movie star can do it, why can't I?" mentality. I hope that's not the case.

I read somewhere a long time ago that the true testament of character is doing the right thing when nobody's watching. I strongly believe in that. I mention this because I believe that being a good person, although perhaps it's sometimes hard for some people, is essential to being happy. Always try to do the right thing, and you'll feel better. That could be the most important advice about being happy in this book: Always try to do the right thing. You'll see. You'll feel better right away, better about yourself and better about life. Then you can try these other little ways to feel happy.

- Try to relax. Try meditation. Simply sitting in a comfortable spot with your eyes closed to clear your mind can give you a sense of peace and calmness. Give yourself some mental breaks during the day, whether it's just taking four long, deep, slow breaths (it works for me) or listening to some soothing music.

  There are countless ways to slow down and relax. Get a professional massage. Look at the stars or clouds for a couple of minutes. Allow yourself to daydream for a bit about something that makes you happy, and let your thoughts wander. Always have a book handy — perhaps one with some poetry or paintings or beautiful photos — and just open it randomly and give it your attention for a little bit before returning to your business of the moment.

- Remember to avoid negative people. With their constant complaints about life, they'll only bring you down to their sense of dissatisfaction.

Unfortunately, there are plenty of these people around, so avoiding them can be difficult. Just try to walk away.

- Be kind. Kindness is never wasted, it doesn't take a lot of effort and it will make a big difference in someone's life. Even if your kindness is not reciprocated, do it again, you never know what kind of trauma, pain or suffering is inside someone's heart. Be generous, giving to charities and helping a fellow human being is a wonderful thing to do. Kindness will not make you weaker, it will make your heart and soul happy. There is not a bad side effect by being kind.

- And another thing: of course, life isn't always peachy. But don't bury your head in the sand whenever problems arise. Postponing inevitable confrontations with your problems is pointless. Instead, try to get them out of the way or solve them as soon as possible. It's always better to keep things out in the open anyway. I admit that this is one department where I still have to do some work myself.

This reminds me of an old story my father used to tell us about a group of gazelles who were grazing happily in the African plains. Suddenly, the gazelles realized that a lion was heading their way. Most of them got the heck out of there, but one chose to simply hide its head in the grass. Lo and behold, the gazelle no longer heard or saw the lion, so it no longer felt afraid. To the gazelle, the lion was not there at all. There was only silence and peace. Well, you can imagine the results. The same is true with life. Ignoring a problem will not make it go away. Eventually, it will catch up with you. The faster you solve the problem, the sooner you can get back to being happy.

- I also always say that there's nothing wrong with enjoying a glass of wine now and then, or in my case, a nice cold glass of champagne. Of course, alcohol or drug abuse is not the way to achieve happiness. I'm sure you've been told many times, but I have witnessed from my piano bench the side effects of such abuse, and they are not fun.

The person usually makes everybody around him or her completely miserable and hurt. When it happens in a public space, you have to add embarrassment to the equation.

- Put as many good thoughts out into the universe as you can and good things will come back to you. Some people call this karma, some call it "good vibrations," some call it love. Whatever you want to call it, thinking warm, positive thoughts about your fellow human beings just might promote a pleasurable feeling of peace and tranquility within you. I try this and I know it makes me feel happy.

- Don't complicate your life. This one is probably easier to say than to do. So many people tend to make things more complicated than they really are.

For example, some days when I go to read my book and get my ice-blended mocha or green tea, I see people who treat ordering a cup of coffee like it is brain surgery or something. These people wait in line for their turn, and when they finally arrive at the counter, they begin to seriously contemplate what they're going to order. When they're with other people, it becomes a sort of "meeting of the minds." I am not kidding. They'll ask each other what to get, or what the other person might get, and then debate their choices like it was a matter of life and death. Then the server will ask what size they want, and it starts all over again: indecision, debate, complications.

My dream is to find a coffee place with a separate window for these people. At that window, you could change your mind every 10 seconds. You could take as much time as you wanted. You could draw up a list of pros and cons for each type of coffee. Whatever, as long as I could zip by to the normal-person window!

I sometimes feel bad for the people behind the counter. They tell me how neurotically some customers behave while doing something as simple as ordering a cup of coffee. Some bombard them with questions: Is it from Sumatra or Colombia? Is it sugar-free, lactose-free, fat-free, gluten-free, caffeine-free, calorie-free? Does it have any additional ingredients harmful to the environment? Do you carry paper straws? On and on. And God forbid the poor guy or girl working there forgets the order.

But these difficult coffee buyers are just one example of many. I wonder, why make things complicated when they don't have to be? Personally, I do not complicate my life. I know what I'd like before it's my turn to order. And if they accidentally mess up my order, I never complain. It's just not that big a deal. Is it really worth it to complicate your life and everyone else's? I don't think so. Get a life!

- Don't live your life in a fantasy land. This is advice that I think a lot of people need to hear. TV, movies, and fiction books are great for entertainment, but they are based in fantasy. Live your own life. Pursue your own dreams and talents. Don't waste your life watching fake people "living" theirs on TV. And don't expect your life to be as dramatic or as glamorous. TV and movies aren't real. Live your own life.

- Take the time, whenever you can, to stop and smell the flowers, literally. I do this quite often. There is something sublime and calming about it. You'd be surprised how rare this simple indulgence is for some people.

- Don't try to change everybody around you. Not everyone will share your outlook on life. I live in Los Angeles and I see what I would call some very weird behavior all the time. But I just shake my head and laugh. Let me tell you a story that I find very funny.

I've mentioned before how I like to read books during my breaks at work. One of the benefits that I enjoyed playing the piano in a mall a few years ago is that I often saw an endless parade of characters walk by. The people that stand out to me the most are perhaps the teenagers, who often interact in strange ways that I have never witnessed anywhere else in the past.

One time — actually, something like this has happened many times — I saw a group of three teenagers sitting at a table at the food court having a juice smoothie. One of their friends then approached the table, and the reaction was over the top. The girls began to shout, "Oh, my *God*! What are you doing here?" The screams of happiness, followed by the embraces and kisses, reminded me of seeing footage on TV of hostages being reunited with their families. It looked like the same overwhelming reactions and emotions. But of course, these kids had just been in the same class together that very same day! I'm sure that they saw each other every day at school and probably even on weekends, but you'd think that they had been trapped somewhere for decades.

I guess it's not that big a deal, just typical teenager stuff. They are young and don't know any better. But to me, it often appears like somebody is one taco short of a combination plate, as they say in my hometown. Maybe one day someone will be able to explain teenagers to me. In the meantime, they are young and having fun, so why would I want to change them or rain on their parade?

- Chocolate. If you like chocolate, and you're not allergic to it, eat it! It will make you feel happy and give you a gentle rush, and, according to many health magazines, it's good for you too. In my humble opinion, chocolate is a vegetable and vegetables are good for you. After all, chocolate comes from cocoa beans. So, they're probably in the same category as green beans, pinto beans, and garbanzo beans, right? Work with me here, dear reader!

- Smile. Laughter and smiling go together. You'll feel happier.

- Be an optimist. I always expect that everything is going to be ok. I think that the result of my endeavors is going to be positive, and if they are not, there is always a next time. When I'm playing tennis, I could be losing 0-5 and 0-40 on my service, one point away from losing the set, but I always think that I will turn the game around. To me, the glass is ALWAYS half full, never half empty. Being an optimistic person, I found myself laughing and making people laugh very often, I would say, every day. My grandmother used to say "Laughter is a medicine with no side effect". The amazing Hellen Keller wrote: "No pessimist ever discovered the secrets of the stars, or sailed to an uncharted land, or opened a new heaven to the human spirit".

- Last but not least: At the end of the day, no matter what kind of day I might have had, I do a little mental exercise. I imagine one of those old-fashioned weight balances, the kind where you put one item on one side and then add a little weight to the other side until the two sides are balanced. I actually still have one of these that used to belong to my mother and grandmother. Using your imagination, place all of the negative parts of your day on one side of the balance. Next, imagine that you're placing all of the blessings you can think of from that same day on the other side of the scale. Personally, I always feel better and happier because, so far, the balance has always tilted towards the happy side. Even when things go wrong, there's just so much to be thankful for. Don't you agree?

I hope you gained something from my thoughts about happiness. Perhaps my philosophy is mostly a result of my strong belief that this business of happiness is my own responsibility and no one else's. Maybe I learned it from the people who have always been around me — my family. In either case, I think my methods work for me. I only hope that some of this will also work for you and that you too will find happiness waiting just around the corner.

If you have the opportunity to listen to my classical CD, it has many of my favorite pieces of music in the classical repertoire. I selected music by Chopin, Liszt, Beethoven, Rachmaninoff, etc., because music has always given me joy and I owe my life to music. I hope that these pieces will caress your heart and massage your soul, as they do for me. Perhaps the combination of this book and the beautiful music can bring you clear skies where all your dreams and aspirations can take flight. I also think that listening to beautiful music while you're driving, can help you to avoid road rage. Many people have told me throughout the years that when there is heavy traffic and they listen to my CD, it has a soothing and calming effect. I think they do have a point.

One final thought. For me, there is one more thing that adds to my wonderful sense of happiness. It's the realization that I have been given the opportunity to live, work, create, and pursue my dreams in the most ambitious and intrinsically unique human experiment in the history of the world, this grand gathering of people of all origins, races, colors, and creeds, this amazing country that I call home, the United States of America. Here, anything and everything is possible. I am the American Dream.

My last two cents about this Happiness "business", love and music are two keys that can help you unlock the doors to a happy place.

In closing, please remember my definition of love: love is helping someone be the best that they can be. I hope that this book and will propel your own true spirit towards that magical place called happiness. Isn't today the perfect time to start that journey?

With loving and happy thoughts,

Antonio Castillo de la Gala

Los Angeles, CA. U.S.A. A.D. 2019

PS: I almost forgot! If you're looking for the answer to the puzzle from Chapter IX, here it is:

Go straight to the box that is labeled "Apples and Oranges." Pick out a fruit. There are only two kinds of fruit in this puzzle, so it will either be an apple or an orange. Now remember, you know that *all three* crates are labeled incorrectly. Since this label says it has both apples and oranges, and you know that each label must be wrong, you can be sure that this crate definitely only contains the type of fruit you picked. If your fruit is an apple, it means you just picked out the crate that has only apples in it (it can't have oranges too, or else the crate's label would be correct). Go ahead and put the "Apple" label on that crate. Simple, right? Now you're almost done.

Now you have two crates left: one used to have the "Apples" sign on it before you put it on its correctly corresponding crate, and the other has the "Oranges" sign on it still. Since you know that all of the original labels were incorrect, you can be sure that crate labeled "Oranges" must have apples *and* oranges in it (the "Apples" label is already taken now!), so put the "Apples and Oranges" label on it instead. Finally, simply take that stray "Oranges" label and place it on the last remaining box. There you go! You solved the puzzle using only the powers of deduction.

Antonio Castillo de la Gala was born in Veracruz, Mexico.

He graduated as a concert pianist from the National Conservatory of Music in Mexico City. Antonio has been a professional pianist in Beverly Hills for 36 years. Besides music, his other passions and loves are family, tennis, books, movies, plays and studying human nature. He has talked about happiness with thousands of relatives, friends, acquaintances and guests before and after performing at concert halls, hotels, schools, shows, restaurants and at private homes. After music, talking about happiness is his greatest love.

He is currently the resident pianist at The Peninsula Hotel in Beverly Hills where he's been performing for more than 10 years, and counting.

He's the happiest person you'll ever meet.

Email: Liszt4you@gmail.com
Instagram: @funwithantonio
Twitter: @ACDLG
Facebook: Antonio Castillo DelaGala
www.antoniocastillodelagala.com

Endorsements

From Veracruz, Mexico to Beverly Hills, USA. A One Shot in a Million story. An immigrant's story about life in the USA, music and happiness. Steps towards achieving happiness. By the time you finished the book, you'll probably feel happier. Fun and true stories that'll entertain you and will give you concrete ideas about feeling and being happy. Get ready to grab the keys to open the gates of happiness. Achieving the American Dream. Antonio IS the American Dream. Antonio has written a must-read book for anyone who wants to find true happiness. His story of growing up with few advantages in his native Mexico and thru his mastery of the piano and love of music finding huge success and popularity entertaining the most powerful people in Hollywood and from around the world is testimony to the power of passion, determination and a positive attitude. He is grateful not just for the success his hard work and talent has brought him but for family, friends and all the little things that bring us happiness every day. things most of us forget to have gratitude for. Antonio's highly readable, teachable book is a reminder to be joyous and grateful and a clear roadmap on how to get there.

Andy Friendly, Emmy nominated television producer and executive, Author: *Willing to be Lucky*

This is really quite a wonderful book — gratitude and happiness. What a winning combination.

John Lescroart, New York Times bestselling author

"What an outstanding and wonderful book! You will find many inspiring episodes about life, gratitude, and joy. It was uplifting to read. This book is the master key that opens the gates of true happiness."

Tetsuya Fukuda, Film maker, screen writer

Antonio's piano genius is a staple among lucky Angelenos. His charisma is transmitted through the ivory placing a personal imprint on classics from Bach to Bernstein. Humble beginnings in Mexico are contrasted with his current life near the gilded streets of Beverly Hills. Antonio's perspective provides a golden nugget of knowledge for his readers. His upbeat book is a didactic treat on how we can all capture and use his easy recipe for happiness.

Vance Owen, Writer, Film Producer

"The road to happiness has many interesting detours. So says Antonio Castillo de la Gala in this charming, wise, anecdote-rich 'ode to joy.' Born in Veracruz, Mexico, he got a grand start in life, with a loving family and a grandmother who began teaching him to play the piano when he was just 3. With determination and a positive attitude, he became a gifted concert pianist and a celebrity performer in many a Los Angeles piano bar. As Antonio relates, one can decide to embrace happiness and kindness and to look on the bright side, even in the face of adversity. Here's his advice, offered with generosity and humor: Seize the day. Drink Champagne. Eat chocolate. And remember that music can caress the heart, calm the soul and delight even the weariest mind.

Martha Groves, Freelance writer and editor and 34-year veteran of the Los Angeles Times

Antonio is a North American treasure. He's a maestro at the piano, with a magnetic personality the size of the ocean. He's a rare and wonderful human being, by any measure!

Allan Durand, winner of the Motion Picture Academy 2012 Nicholl Award in Screenwriting.

"This book is like having a good cup of coffee with a dear friend who wants to let you in on why he's in such a good mood. Only, this friend is in a good mood ALL THE TIME. Once you start reading, you will begin to hear Antonio's voice in your head, and you will find yourself nodding along, chuckling as you go, listening to his philosophy of unbridled optimism... and its roots in his inspiring personal story. A gifted pianist from Mexico, Antonio is someone who does more than embody the American dream, he broadcasts it with his every word and deed. Like the antidote to the poison of cynicism, drink up Antonio's words on happiness — they will leave you feeling full of joy and gratitude."

Patricia Beauchamp, Screenwriter